W9-BYU-524

Saint Peter's University Library
Withdrawn

TWAYNE'S WORLD AUTHORS SERIES

A Survey of the World's Literature

Sylvia E. Bowman, Indiana University

GENERAL EDITOR

AUSTRALIA

Joseph Jones, University of Texas

EDITOR

Kenneth Slessor

(TWAS 145)

TWAYNE'S WORLD AUTHORS SERIES (TWAS)

The purpose of TWAS is to survey the major writers—novelists, dramatists, historians, poets, philosophers, and critics—of the nations of the world. Among the national literatures covered are those of Australia, Canada, China, Eastern Europe, France, Germany, Greece, India, Italy, Japan, Latin America, New Zealand, Poland, Russia, Scandinavia, Spain, and the African nations, as well as Hebrew, Yiddish, and Latin Classical literatures. This survey is complemented by Twayne's United States Authors Series and English Authors Series.

The intent of each volume in these series is to present a critical analytical study of the works of the writer; to include biographical and historical material that may be necessary for understanding, appreciation, and critical appraisal of the writer; and to present all material in clear, concise English—but not to vitiate the scholarly content of the work by doing so.

Kenneth Slessor

By HERBERT C. JAFFA

New York University

Twayne Publishers, Inc.   ::   New York

Copyright © *1971 by Twayne Publishers, Inc.*
All Rights Reserved

Library of Congress Catalog Card Number: 73-120507

MANUFACTURED IN THE UNITED STATES OF AMERICA

Preface

I read my first Australian verse at Darley, an Australian army camp near the lovely village of Bacchus Marsh some miles inland from the port of Melbourne. It was the summer of 1942, and we had come there after crossing a month of southern ocean from San Francisco. We were to have ten days at Darley before scattering northward to war, and when we weren't writing "V" letters home, drinking the fine Australian beer, or exploring the beautiful clumps of green hills with white sheep, some of us discovered "a jolly swagman camped by a billabong/ Under the shade of a coolibah tree."

We were to meet the jolly swagman of "Waltzing Matilda" many times during the next two years, often in verses other than those composed by A. B. ("Banjo") Paterson and not always appropriate for the family dining room. We listened to and sang the folk ballad as we moved northward—from Townsville, North Queensland, along the Great Barrier Reef, to Port Moresby in New Guinea, over the Owen Stanley Range into Buna, Dubadura, Markham Valley, and Lae.

I relate the circumstances of this early contact with Australian verse because, from them, colored by memory, came the impulse years later to study the literature of Australia. The present volume on Kenneth Slessor is one expression of that study.

In retrospect I can see that the ballads of Paterson and others had been particularly meaningful. They had not only given me some sense of the spirit which still touched the Australian people, but also, in doing so, had led me to the poems of the more serious and imaginative Australian poets; Kenneth Slessor is perhaps the most significant of these poets.

Slessor's significance is both historical and absolute. He is a pioneer in the development of modern Australian poetry, and he is a poet of distinctly individual poems of power and beauty. This study pays attention to Slessor as a spokesman for the modern movement, particularly as it relates to the liberation of Australian poetry from parochialism. But my primary purpose in the volume is to introduce and discuss the poems of a remarkable poet who is almost completely unknown in the United States. Biographical and historical information are included to place Slessor in the contemporary scene as well as against the background of the Australian literary tradition. This, however, together with the critical analysis, is subordinated to serve the poem. Similarly, the body of Slessor criticism is selectively used rather than discussed at length. Diffused throughout the book, the criticism is brought forward when necessary to help reveal the poem and allow the poem to reveal the poet.

In general, the poems are presented in chronological order of their composition and publication in three different collections. The major poems are discussed and quoted at length; the minor ones receive briefer treatment except where they have an importance in the development of the poet. In some instances poems are quoted more extensively than they would be if the original text material were available to the American reader.

I did not come to the poetry of Kenneth Slessor until after the war, though during the war I had heard of his work as a newspaperman; he had served as a correspondent with the Australian forces at Finschhaven, New Guinea, not too far from the Nadzab-Markham Valley area where I was located. Mr. Slessor and I have never met, but in connection with this volume we have written to each other and I acknowledge here his graciousness.

HERBERT C. JAFFA

Manhasset, New York

Acknowledgments

I gratefully acknowledge the permission of Angus & Robertson Ltd. of Sydney, Australia, to quote extensively from Kenneth Slessor's *Poems*. I acknowledge further the publisher's kindness over the years in providing me, unsolicited, with many volumes of poetry and prose; without them it would have been difficult, from this distance, to have kept informed about developments in Australian literature. In this connection and with other assistance related to the preparation of this present volume, I am particularly grateful to Senior Editor John D. Abernethy.

To John Vaughan, Librarian at the Office of the Australian Consulate General in New York and to Pauline Fanning, the Australian Reference Librarian at the National Library at Canberra, I express my deep appreciation; without their labors in my behalf in locating, photostating, and sending materials to me, it would have been difficult to complete this book.

A note of thanks must be directed also to one of Australia's great bibliophiles, Walter Stone of Cremorne, New South Wales. Hearing, secondhand, of my need to examine an important paper, he sent one of his two remaining copies to me. He also advised me of additional sources of information which proved useful to this study. Mr. Stone's interest and generosity were typical of the many people throughout Australia upon whom I called for assistance. One such person is Alison Dolling of the South Australia Teachers Association. I am indebted to her not only for searching out and sending material to me, but also for encouraging a dialogue about teaching and Australian poetry.

Jack Lindsay, writing from England, clarified for me some of the things he had said about Slessor and the *Vision* days in his autobiography, *The Roaring Twenties*. And C. Hartley Grattan, writing from the University of Texas, helped with a little "shoptalk" about Australian poetry as well as providing me with copies of some needed periodicals from the valuable Grattan Collection.

Finally, I thank my wife, Edith, for helping me prepare the manuscript of this study for publication.

Contents

In the sharp sky, the frosty deepnesses,
There are still birds to barb the silences,
There are still fields to meet the morning on,
But those who made them beautiful have gone.
                                    Slessor, "The Country Ride"

For the family of Harry Dinsmore
who lived in Townsville, North
Queensland, Australia.

Chronology

1901   Kenneth Slessor born March 27, 1901, in the town of Orange, New South Wales. Father, Robert, metallurgist and mining engineer, born in England. Mother, Margaret, born in Australia.

1908- Visited England with parents.
1910

1910- Educated at Mowbray House School, Chatswood, New
1919   South Wales, and the North Shore Church of England Grammar School in Sydney.

1920- Worked as a reporter on the *Sydney Sun.*
1924

1922   Married Noela Senior.

1923- Jointly edited and contributed to *Vision: A Literary*
1924   *Quarterly,* in which some of the first poems were published. Co-edited *Poetry in Australia 1923,* an anthology published by the Vision Press. Published *Thief of the Moon* in an edition limited to one hundred signed copies.

1926   Published *Earth-Visitors,* largely a reprint of *Thief of the Moon.*

1925   Served as chief subeditor with the *Melbourne Punch* and a feature writer with the *Melbourne Herald.*

1926   Returned to Sydney as special writer for the *Sydney Sun.*

1927- Joined staff of *Smith's Weekly* in Sydney. Was to become
1939   its associate editor in 1936, editor in 1938, and editor-in-chief of Smith's newspapers in 1939.

1931   September 17 Declared for "Modernism" in an address, "Experiments in Modern English Poetry" before the Australian English Association. Collaborated with two other poets on *Trio: A Book of Poems,* which included "Five Visions of Captain Cook."

1932   Published *Cuckooz Contrey;* also a volume of light verse, *Darlinghurst Nights and Early Morning Glories,* which collected some of the verse written as part of his regular responsibility at *Smith's Weekly*.

1939   Published *Five Bells*.

1940-   Appointed Australian official war correspondent and
1944   served in the United Kingdom, Greece, Palestine, Syria, Egypt, and New Guinea. Last important poem, "Beach Burial," came out of war experience.

1944-   Rejoined the *Sydney Sun*, becoming chief leader-writer
1957   and literary editor.

1944   Published *One Hundred Poems 1919-1939*. This volume is significant in that it represents a bringing together by Australia's major publisher, Angus and Robertson, of all the poems previously collected in *Five Bells* (1939), *Cuckooz Contrey* (1932), and twenty-five of the thirty-six poems in *Earth-Visitors* (1926). These earlier volumes, beautifully printed with woodcuts and etchings, were usually published in limited editions. *One Hundred Poems* subsequently was reprinted in 1947 and 1951. November 23, appealed for "literary values" by which to judge Australian poetry rather than "historical or sentimental" ones, in twenty-first anniversary address before the Australian English Association.

1945   Death of wife. Edited the anthology *Australian Poetry, 1945*.

1951   Married Pauline Wallace. Son born 1952.

1953   Appointed member of the Advisory Board of the Commonwealth Literary Fund.

1954   Delivered ten lectures on Australian poetry at University of Sydney.

1956-   President of the Sydney Journalists' Club.
1964

1956-   Accepted editorship of *Southerly* (with *Meanjin*, one of
1961   the two more important literary magazines in Australia).

1957-   Left the *Sydney Sun* to become leader-writer and book
1969   reviewer for the *Sydney Daily Telegraph*.

1957   Published *Poems* (essentially a reissue of *One Hundred Poems* with three additional poems).

1958   Co-edited (one of three editors) *The Penguin Book of Modern Australian Verse*.

Chronology

1959   Appointed an officer of the Order of the British Empire (O.B.E.) for "services to Australian literature."

1961   Second marriage dissolved.

1968   Appointed member of National Literature Board of Review.

CHAPTER I

The Man and the Setting: An Introduction

K ENNETH SLESSOR is a major Australian poet, some of whose poems are among the most important written in English in modern literature. Now in his late sixties, he is probably the best known poet of his generation in Australia, and his verse provides the staple of almost every anthology of modern and contemporary Australian poetry. As the island-continent has moved upright out of its "cultural cringe"[1] and toward an appreciation of its own literature, Slessor has become a "poet of the classroom," and his work is read and studied as part of secondary school and college and university curricula. Perhaps this is an unexpected role for the poet of gaiety who in his youth sent "Good roistering easy maids, blown cock-a-hoop/On floods of tavern-steam"[2] to help heal the hurt of Gallipoli. Published shortly after World War I, Slessor's first poems, adorned with barebreasted mermaids and nudes astride gamboling centaurs, "were read with a quickening delight as symbols of youth resurgent from the mire and the wreckage."[3] But the classroom role may not be inappropriate for the mature poet who spoke in new language of the land and its legend and the Wasteland of men's lives.

I Growth of Reputation

Between World War I and World War II Kenneth Slessor spoke to his countrymen of their discoverer, Cook, the "captain with the sad/And fine white face, who never lost a man/Or flinched a peril."[4] And he recalled for them their history and revived for them their myth. And to a people mostly huddled in teeming cities he spoke with affection, for their "red globes of light, the liquor-green,/The pulsing arrows and the running fire/Spilt on the stone" and for the "Smells rich and rasping,

smoke and fat . . ./And puffs of paraffin that crimp the nose."[5]
But he spoke to them also of the beauty and horror of the heart
of their land, where "nothing . . . moves" and "the sky lies empty"
and "the sun is as white as moonlight."[6] And for some of his
countrymen he returned to them an image of themselves they
had lost related to a land they had loved.

Yet, perhaps as meaningful, the older Slessor, "the poet of
beauty and cruelty," also spoke above his land, spoke to the
question of modern man: the meaning of his living and the fact
of his ceasing to be. "If I could find an answer," he cried out to
a friend long dead, "could only find/Your meaning, or could
say why you were here/Who now are gone, what purpose gave
you breath/Or seized it back, might I not hear your voice?" (106)
To the extent that Kenneth Slessor is known at all to Americans,
it is probably through the poem "Five Bells," from which these
lines are quoted. The American poet-critic, Selden Rodman first
included it twenty years ago in his anthology, *One Hundred
Modern Poems,* a collection of "the best in modern poetry,"[7]
and the anthology has been reprinted at least a dozen times since.

Most of Slessor's verse, even the first poems, are worth reading:
his use of language engages one almost at once. But, by and
large, it is the later poems like "Five Bells," written between
1927 and 1939, and a last one, "Beach Burial," which grew out
of his war correspondent experience in Egypt, for which he is
best known.

It was a sympathetic Australian critic almost a decade ago
who noted that although contemporary *littérateurs* hardly read
Slessor anymore, no university course that might be developed
on Australian literature could fail to take him into account as
"one of the most important figures." Yet, the critic was somewhat
saddened by that fact: for it was "ironical that the least academic
of our poets, the one who most consistently has spoken in simple
earnestness to common men and women, has every appearance
of becoming a dead object, ready for some curriculum."[8]

Today, the poems of Kenneth Slessor have, indeed, become
part of some curriculum, as well as part of the reading matter
of an increasing number of people in the general community.
But, by no means, can the poems be termed dead objects. Rather,
they have excited new interest and inquiry. This seems particularly true among the students, hundreds of whom write to

Slessor each year, and with whom, through his letters and writings in the *Sydney Daily Telegraph*, Slessor has conducted an occasional dialogue. He is sympathetic to the students "whose fate it is to have to wrestle with [my poems]—a situation, I would have foreseen with horror in the days when I toiled at school myself, cursing the authors of the set pieces."[9]

But if Kenneth Slessor, nearing seventy, remains a most "alive" poet—and not only for the students but for a widening circle of adult readers for whom his poems are now more accessible than they were when first published—he is much less alive, in fact, seems almost a shade, to many of Australia's *littérateurs:* to them he is at best a presence rather than a poet and they have placed his poems in Australia's literary past.

This is understandable for *littérateurs,* for Slessor has become a private poet who has not published a new poem in almost a quarter of a century. In fact, his *One Hundred Poems* (1944) in which he brought together three collections of verse written between 1919 and 1939, now seems to have been his final poetic statement. Yet "Beach Burial," conceived during the war near El Alamein in 1942, and one of the last three poems he published after his return to Australia, does provide a meaningful postscript.

II *Poet versus Journalist*

To most Australian critics, Slessor has been silent these many years because he "no longer has anything to say."[10] One critic, speaking of his work, says that the poet, with "Five Bells," his final triumph, "has made his world fully articulate and has thus set the seal upon his small but distinguished *oeuvre*."[11] Another, speaking of his person, says that "everything that went to make up the poet in Slessor conspired to make him put down his pen forever."[12] Slessor, himself, contemplates these poetically empty years and says, "If I could only get away for a year or so, I'd resume writing poetry."[13]

This more pedestrian explanation (as against the poetic and psychological one) should not be dismissed out of hand. Slessor *has* been very busy and *has not* been able "to get away for a year or two." Though not a practicing poet now for almost a quarter of a century, he has been for twice that time, and continues to be to the present, a "very" practicing newspaperman, "one of [Australia's] all-time great journalists."[14] Whether or not it was newspaper work that constituted the "hell" from which Slessor early took refuge in the writing of poetry—for him, "a pleasure out of hell"[15]—it is nonetheless true that the poet, all his working life, has chosen journalism to be his first responsibility.

If Slessor's first published poem (at the age of fifteen in the *Sydney Bulletin*)[16] preceded his first published newspaper story, it was almost the last time that it would. For, from the beginning in 1920 when at age nineteen he joined the *Sydney Sun* as a cub reporter, to his present eminence as doyen of Sydney journalists, leader writer for the *Sydney Daily Telegraph*, and past President of the prestigious Sydney Journalists' Club, Kenneth Slessor's primary and abiding commitment has been to journalism.

From the vantage point of today, there seems little question that, as a young reporter caught up in the bohemian life of the Roaring Twenties in Sydney, Slessor very much did want to write poetry and "was already chafing against the journalist yoke, afraid that he would never be able to liberate all his powers with the daily grind of reporting."[17] Yet, simultaneously, unlike his fellow poets, Slessor would not commit his all to bohemia and the Muse. "He was doing well as a journalist," a poet and a friend of the time was to remember in his autobiography, "and had nothing of my hankering for hardship as a test of devotion."[18]

Slessor would not disagree. Himself, looking back to those exhilarating days when he began publishing his first poems in *Vision*, the Dionysian-inspired quarterly designed to "[liberate] the imagination by gaiety or fantasy,"[19] Slessor has recalled that he really "wasn't part of [the Bohemian world] . . . though a very amused and detached observer . . . I didn't belong to it, mainly because I'd committed the unpardonable offence and got myself a steady job at £4/10/0 a week, which put me beyond the pale."[20]

Kenneth Slessor was to seek the steady job and remain a part-time poet all his life. He became a newspaperman's newspaperman, a gifted "doer of anything . . . the [journalistic] gods wished to dump on him,"[21] rising rapidly from the ranks to become editor-in-chief of *Smith's Weekly* and other Smith newspapers, and chief leader-writer and literary editor of the *Sydney*

Sun, before assuming his present senior position with the *Sydney Daily Telegraph.* That Slessor could have been a greater poet if he had not "[stuck] to his journalistic career,"[22] as Jack Lindsay, his co-editor on *Vision,* would have it, is, of course possible. Yet, Slessor's newspaper fans, and there are many, could point with equal vigor to the connection between Slessor's training and high sense of professionalism as a journalist, and the discipline and high standards he set for himself as a part-time poet, the dedication to which was to make him "the finest craftsman of them all."[23]

Almost simultaneously, as Slessor the full-time newspaperman matured and learned his craft, so, too, did Slessor the part-time poet. And as his finely wrought stories and editorials made their appearance, together with "fancifully humorous articles, more entertaining than anything of the sort in the Australia of his generation,"[24] so, too, did his splendid and precise "new" poetry; all of Australian poetry was to be influenced by it and raised "to a new level of intellectual responsibility . . . ending once for all the reign of the slipshod, the pedestrian and the emotionally-inchoate."[25]

III *Separately Published Volumes*

Between 1926 and early 1940, when he was appointed Australian official war correspondent, Slessor published the three collections upon which his reputation currently rests as a major poet in the modern tradition. The first, *Earth-Visitors* (1926), includes several poems which, though meaningful in themselves, contribute most in helping us to locate and take pleasure in the early burgeoning of the later Slessor. Some of the poems also allow us to share vicariously in a short-lived but significant cultural "crusade" of the twenties that sought to dilute the parochialism of Australian poetry. The crusade, somewhat unclear in its philosophical accompaniment of nature worship and Greek mythology, was very clear in what it stood for: "Good poetry is based on clear images, and subject matter should not be local, but should come from worlds worked by the imagination."[26]

The poetry that the crusade sent forth, and Slessor's was best, by far, must have seemed strange to readers of the time who equated poetry with bush ballads like "Waltzing Matilda" or with nationalistic strivings: "Great Australia is not yet: She waits/Where o'er the Bush prophetic auras play."[27] This is not to suggest that a great number of people were either caught up in the crusade or even read Slessor's early poems when they first appeared in *Vision* magazine in 1923, the *Vision* anthology in 1924, or afterward in *Earth-Visitors*. But, in terms of the time, many did, particularly the *littérateurs*, and were startled by a poetry filled with new feeling and meaning evoked by new sound and imagery. Who were these "Earth-Visitors," these "strange riders . . . [who] came gusting down/Cloaked in dark furs, with faces grave and sweet,/And white as air"? And what did "those tumbling babes of heaven,/Plump cherubim with blown cheeks" or "Those friends of Lao-Tzu, those wise old men/Dozing all day in lemon-silken robes,/With tomes of beaten jade spread knee to knee," have to do with Australia?[28]

Clement Semmler, the Australian literary editor and biographer, suggests that Slessor's early verse had an "impact on the antipodally-removed readers of the 1920s [that] was as unexpected, jarring and yet stimulating as Eliot's early poetry elsewhere."[29] Certainly, after *Earth-Visitors* a new horizon of imagination seems to have been extended for the reader and a new encouragement offered the poet to seek new possibilities in language and form. But it is less to *Earth-Visitors* which, in retrospect, is seen primarily as the promise, and much more to the flowering in *Cuckooz Contrey* (1932) and *Five Bells* (1939) that Slessor owes his significance.

To his country's greatest literary historian, H. M. Green, it was through *Cuckooz Contrey* that "the first wave of modernism in verse—the verse represented by T. S. Eliot . . ."[30] was to reach Australia. And to one of Australia's best contemporary poets and editors, Douglas Stewart, it is the poem, "The Five Visions of Captain Cook," in the *Cuckooz* volume, that provided "the most dramatic break-through into the [Australian] poetry of the twentieth century." An exploration into the discoverer of a nation, the "Cook" poem "was to give much of the impetus to a whole series of 'voyager poems' and explorer poems of great power and stature and significance."[31]

Five Bells was to prove equally important. Not only was it to offer in its title poem "one of the two or three best poems written in Australia,"[32] but also it was to signal Slessor's emergence as one of the earliest poets to deal with the life of the city. His concern with Sydney stimulated an interest in urban life as a subject of poetry, and his wryly critical "essentially urban"[33] attitude to the Australian countryside sounded a note which continues to be echoed in much of contemporary Australian verse.

Within some months after the publication of *Five Bells,* Slessor the part-time poet became the full-time war correspondent. He served a good war, covering with distinction the allied retreat and the surrender of Syria in 1941, the fierce seesaw battle for North Africa in 1942, and the Australian-American landings at Finschhaven and Cape Gloucester in New Guinea in 1943. His reports from the field, describing with the utmost honesty, clarity, and restrained compassion the life and death of the Australian soldier, made Slessor's a household name throughout Australia. His reports were looked at, clipped, and held, and some still are, as an account of the darkest days in Australian history.

In 1944, after a disagreement with the Australian army authorities over his account of a battle in New Guinea, he resigned his commission. "I am bitterly disappointed," Slessor said at the time, "that I am now forced to give up the struggle to tell in my own way the story of Australian fighting men for whom I have so deep an admiration."[34] This need to tell the story "in my own way," the respect for self and craft, a concern for the personal and precise rendering of an experience—these are no less typical of Slessor the poet than they are of Slessor the newspaperman.

IV   *The Post-War Years*

But if Slessor the newspaperman had returned from the wars, Slessor the poet had not. The year of his return he published what was essentially to be his definitive volume. In *One Hundred Poems* (1944) he brought together twenty-five of the thirty-six early poems in *Earth-Visitors* and all of the later ones in *Cuckooz Contrey* and *Five Bells* and carefully organized them in three separate sections to indicate their date of composition. From that point on, Slessor was to publish just three more short poems

SAINT PETER'S COLLEGE LIBRARY
JERSEY CITY, NEW JERSEY 07306

(a total of thirty lines) and then lapse into silence that has now extended into almost a quarter of a century.

Despite the absence of new poems, Slessor's popularity, based on the old ones, continues to grow. Certainly this is suggested by the many reprintings of *One Hundred Poems* and, in recent years, reprintings with increasing frequency and in larger editions. Since its first publication in 1944, *One Hundred Poems* has been reprinted twice, in 1947 and 1951, under its original title and then, beginning in 1957, under the title *Poems*, which embraced the three short poems Slessor wrote after the war. *Poems* itself then was reprinted half-dozen times and in paperback edition: in 1963, twice in 1964, and once in each of the years, 1966, 1967, and 1968. Another printing is scheduled for 1970-1971. In recent years there even has been a brief renewal of some critical attention paid to Slessor. Pointed primarily at the general reader and student who have come only lately to his poems, articles about Slessor and his work have appeared separately in pamphlet form and as chapters and parts of chapters in an increasing number of books on Australian literature, culture, tradition, and mores.[35]

Of course, the essential reason for Slessor's popularity lies in his poetry, and a critical analysis of it is the first concern of this study. Yet, the nonpublishing poet's continual visibility as an important newspaperman (a leader-writer and literary editor) has contributed also to people's knowing about him, remembering and wanting to read his poems. So too has Slessor's continued involvement in and support of literary projects and publications designed to help in the development of poetry in Australia.

From 1956 to 1961 Slessor served as a part-time editor of the prestigious literary journal *Southerly* and in 1958 was one of three editors of the widely distributed *Penguin Book of Modern Australian Verse*. In 1953 he accepted membership on the Advisory Board of the Commonwealth Literary Fund, a major source of financial support for Australia's major literary magazines and the provider of grants, fellowships, and subsidies to writers and publishers. These activities and his appointment by Queen Elizabeth in 1959 as an officer of the Order of the British Empire (O.B.E.) for "service to Australian literature," have helped to reinforce Slessor's presence and meaning for many people; this, despite his "absence" as an active poet.

V   *Reasons for Continuing Popularity*

A modest and retiring man, Slessor is at the same time an accessible one who will answer questions and talk about his work. There is an appropriateness in that the frontispiece of the anthology, *Australian Poets Speak* (1961),[36] is of Slessor. Standing before a desk, a book in his left hand, his right knuckled down to emphasize a point, the poet is depicted as discussing one of three poems from *Earth-Visitors* and *Cuckooz Contrey* included in the anthology.

Slessor is also a cultured man with a large knowledge of and deep feeling for literature and music. Yet, he is not an academic, as are several of his peers; in fact, he has shown no enthusiasm at all for the academic posture or the academic laurel. Nevertheless, he has been and continues to be a willing and successful lecturer at the university. His interest, however, remains essentially with the student and the student's efforts to understand and appreciate.

All this—Slessor's competence, character, and visibility—have contributed to his popularity. But the fact that more people than ever before are reading his poems, is due also, and significantly so, to the general rise in the level of education. Most Australians are much better educated today than they were when Slessor started publishing a half-century ago. Unlike the time of the poet's youth, very few of today's youngsters, among Slessor's most appreciative readers, will not graduate from high school; an increasing number, in fact, will go on to the university. And here, too, in higher education, there has been a dramatic change upward. Before the outbreak of World War II, there were only six universities in the entire country. Now there are at least twice that number and the student population has risen from 15,000 to about 75,000. Certainly these changes add up to a growing number of literate readers with a willingness to read poetry and consequently more Australian publishers with a willingness to publish it.

But perhaps the most important reason for Slessor's contemporaneity is the spirit of the times in Australia. As suggested by the support for Australian studies in the schools—the first Chair in Australian Literature, founded at the University of Sydney in 1961, was financed by *public* subscription—and by the large number of publications dealing with the exploration of the continent, the development of the nation, and the culture of the people, there is a revived interest in the Australian experience, both collective and individual. In such an atmosphere it is natural that Slessor should be rediscovered and read. Is he not, after all, the pioneer poet of modern Australian poetry, the poet who "is required reading for anyone who would understand the hows and the whys of [Australian] poetry since it first shook off the uniform of colonialism at its most grotesque in the late 1920s and early 1930s"?[37]

Yet, here too, Kenneth Slessor is not read simply because he is a pioneer, a presence, or an important figure in the history of Australian literature. His poetry has become "required reading" because he remains today "the finest craftsman of them all," the absolute poet who speaks in splendid language and "in simple earnestness to common men and women."[38] In this day of Australian rediscovery, of land and of self, Slessor is read with increasing appreciation because he is both the explorer, Cook, who sailed westward "Over the brink into the devil's mouth" to find Australia, and the explorer, Man, who between the double ding-dong and the single ding of a ship's "Five Bells," sought his own soul.

Slessor's is an Australian voice, but one that speaks also to contemporary man without relationship to country. And if Slessor's courage in breaking new ground in language and form has cast him in the role of a pioneer in the development of modern Australian poetry, it has no less earned him the role of a forerunner in modern verse in general, and a linkage with Eliot, Yeats, Owen, and Edith Sitwell—all of whom have meaning for him. Yet, if Slessor's poetry is to be fully appreciated, he must be seen also as an inheritor. And his inheritance is not only of the strong and prevailing English cultural tradition, but also of the Australian response to that tradition. For behind Slessor's *One Hundred Poems* is 150 years of Australian struggle for selfhood.

VI *Slessor's Predecessors: Earlier Australian Verse*

Kenneth Slessor was born in 1901 at Orange, New South Wales, the first settled of the six Australian states. The year is important because on New Year's Day of that year Australia was proclaimed a nation. The place is important because nearby was the birthplace of A. B. "Banjo" Paterson, the greatest of the Australian bush balladists. All three—Slessor, the imaginative poet, Australia, finally a nation, and the bush balladists—are interrelated.

The link between the bush balladist and the unfurling of the new Australian flag on the first day of the new century was a close one. For the flag, which balanced the Southern Cross against the British Union Jack and the six-pointed white star of the new unified six Australian states, symbolized a "marriage" between old British values and new indigenous ones that had emerged from a century of struggle with a strange and harsh continent. The bush balladists had been a very important part of that struggle. No people could become a nation nor "could live a full life . . . or indeed live in any real sense at all until it began to seek imaginative expression for its thoughts and feelings."[39] In the 1880s and, more dramatically in the nineties with "Banjo" Paterson, the bush balladists provided this expression.

Helped by a vigorous oral literautre that had grown out of the folk songs and English-Scotch ballads of the earlier settlers, the balladists embraced the heartland of the country, the bush or outback, and the people who lived and worked there. They wrote ballads about sheep shearers and stockmen and station hands and squatters. And they wrote of "mateship born in barren lands,/Of toil and thirst and danger."[40] They discovered "the law of the Overland that all in the West obey—/A man must cover with travelling sheep a six-mile stage a day."[41] And they found also "a jolly swagman camped by a billabong,/Under the shade of a coolibah tree, [who] sang, as he watched . . . while his billy boiled, 'Who'll come a-waltzing Matilda with me?' "[42]

The balladists wrote about actual men and actual conditions, but their verses also provided the possibilities for myth-building, necessary to a people forming a nation. "Saltbush Bill" and "Clancy of the Overflow" were more than just popular ballads; their heroes, as those in "The Man from Snowy River" and "The Man from Ironbark," became familiar and personal figures to people in all parts of the country. Their exploits, at first read (in fact, recited out loud) in shearers' huts and campfires or along the dusty miles of cattle trails, gradually became standard fare for the city dweller.

As people increasingly concentrated in the few cities, a concentration which, by Slessor's birth in 1901, was to include a third of the population, they had an increasing need to identify with an image that seemed distinctly Australian. The city, crowded and mean and "cant-ridden," seemed second hand and European and "limped," as Sydney, in particular did, "in apish imitation after London ideas, habits, and manners."[43] It was the outback, depicted by "Banjo" Paterson and the other balladists, which offered the city dweller "the most distinctly [and most idealistic] Australian types of life and scene to be found on the continent."[44] And it was with the Australian of the outback, tough, irreverent of authority, mildly ironical, and always loyal to his mates, with whom he identified. The outback and its people, revealed in ballads sometimes crude in form but usually lyrical in voice, provided the unifying image for most Australians as they moved toward nationhood and beyond.

This image or Australian "self-picture," once so crucial to a peoples' growth, lingered for a long time; it remains, though somewhat blurred, even today. Certainly over the years popular Australian literature did little to dissolve it. The Australian novel, which emerged toward the turn of the century, remained preoccupied through the thirties with the life and landscape of the bush or outback—and this at a time when 85 percent of the population was already living in towns and cities. And, if in the poetry before World War I a few imaginative bards sang their personal songs without reference to the bush, they sang them to almost a silent audience. It was, in fact, precisely in rebellion against the persistence of the Australian "image" and its dull reflection in the nationalism and parochialism of Australian poetry, that the *Vision* crusade, in which Slessor was an important participant, developed. "Subject matter should not be local," the crusaders said, "but should come from worlds evoked by the imagination."[45]

"From worlds evoked by imagination"—a liberating message in the 1920s for the poet limited to the horizons of his land. Yet a shackling one for the Australian poet of a century before. He had still to discover and deal with his new land, and "worlds evoked by imagination" would take him from the land and blind him to its beauty. For, in the early 1800s, the imagination of the Australian poet was imprisoned by visions of the English countryside and surfeited by the rich heritage of English literature. The struggle of the early poets in Australia was to achieve a "parochialism" and to identify with this most ancient of continents: to learn how to translate the land and the life in its *own* terms, not English ones. The struggle was to be a long one, echoing into Slessor's youth and in the struggle, the later efforts of Paterson and the bush balladists can be seen as significant not only in that they helped to create an "Australian image," but also in that they helped the imaginative poet feel at home with his land.

If not the "poet" in the traditional sense, certainly the popular "versifier" was present almost from the beginning: from the departure of the First Fleet from England in May 1787, to the disembarking in the virgin bush at Sydney Cove in January, 1788, and the establishment of the Penal Colony. "Farewell to old England for ever," lamented the anonymous bard, "Farewell to our rum-culls as well;/Farewell to the well-loved Old Bailey/ Where I used for to cut such a swell."[46]

The Crown had intended no nation to ultimately emerge with flapping flags in 1901 when it transported a wretched band of convicts to Sydney Cove in 1787. And no sense of the high purpose or mission that had accompanied the start of Cook's voyage of discovery twenty years before, was present when the First Fleet set sail with a thousand convicts and their jailers. The convicts and New Holland, as Australia was then called, was simply part of the Crown's plan "to remove the inconvenience which arose from the crowded state of the gaols." American independence in 1783 had cut off the colonies as a dumping ground for England's surplus convicts, and the Crown, until their removal, had "crammed [them] into 'temporary' accommodations in hulks moored in the Thames estuary and at Portsmouth."[47]

Such was the beginning of Australia—a place of exile, "a convict colony established for sordid and expedient reasons."[48] Certainly this promised little toward the development of an independent nation; even less toward the development of an indigenous Australian poetry which would embrace the land. Those who came in chains had no reason to glory in and celebrate Australia. Nor did the first free settlers who came afterward, especially under "assisted immigration"[49] in the 1830s: they came to exploit the land, not to nourish it, and the land was harsh and took its toll.

This is not to say that in the early days there was no creative or almost "poetic" response to the uniqueness of Australia. The anonymous early verses and songs reflect not only a looking-back to England, but a consciousness of and sensitivity to the special aspects of the new land. Very early, for example, transplanted Englishmen from the slums of London discovered the bush and the aborigines, and the melody in the aboriginal place names:

> Cabramatta, Bogolong,
> Ulladulla, Gerringong,
> If you wouldn't become an orang-outang,
> Don't go to the wilds of Australia.[50]

For the poet and more serious and imaginative writer of verse, the response to the new land came later and involved with it a long process of identification and perception. The fact of "exile" and ultimately of "being a colonist" in Australia, was to prove a large obstacle to the poet's development and the growth of a truly Australian poetry. In the beginning, the colonial poet saw the Australian scene only in terms of that literary and cultural tradition with which he was familiar: the English one. To reconcile poetically what he saw with what he knew was impossible.

For how could the poet have used Augustan rhetoric and the polished couplets of Pope to translate the boisterous crudity of the colony? And how could he have recorded the primitive wildness and the "age-unbroken silence" of the Australian bush with the language of Wordsworth and Tennyson, expressive of an English society and a countryside humanized for centuries? "There were traditional terms to describe oaks and deer," poet-educator T. Inglis Moore reminds us, "but none to grapple with the gum-tree or cope with the kangaroo."[51]

Slessor and the *Vision* poets were later to liberate a parochial poetry by replacing the then omnipresent native kookaburra with a Greek satyr. But the task of the early colonial poet was first to learn how to use and make poetry out of this loud laughing bird—and out of the cockatoo, wallaby, and mopoke, and out of "different" words like *cooee* and *coolibah, billabong* and *bunya*. If the people had already made Cabramatta and Gerringong part of their song, it was the poet's task to try to make them part of his sonnet. "The creation of a suitable diction to reveal [his] antipodean world"—this was to be his struggle.[52]

That much of the nineteenth century Australian poetry, reflecting this struggle—was self-conscious, imitative, and often crude in form, is less surprising than the fact that some authentically poetic and indigenous voices were heard. One belonged to Charles Harpur, (1813-1868), the son of convict parents, who began publishing in the 1840s. Born in the beautiful valley of the Hawkesbury River in New South Wales, and self-educated in the traditional idiom, especially of Milton and Wordsworth, Harpur experimented with words, images, and meter to more precisely describe his deep feelings for the landscape. His poems, obviously derivative and frequently forced and verbose, nevertheless captured for the first time the atmosphere of the Australian bush, particularly its play of light, breathless heat, stillness, and solitude.

Another voice, a superior one, was Henry Kendall's. If Harpur's poetry was the important pioneer effort to adapt the traditional idiom to serve the Australian environment, Kendall's poetry bore the fruit of that effort. Inspired by Harpur, Kendall (1839-1882), publishing in the 1860s, responded directly to the landscape and found the language to express the uniqueness of the experience. More than any poet before him, he sang naturally of the land beneath the Southern Cross. Intellectually aware of the "West wind full of birds' cries" and of "primrose tufts and grown bower," emotionally he felt only the "dry winds [that] hiss" and saw only the "mulga and salt bush shrubs." And if delighted by the English skylarks, he loved more "the silver-voiced bell-birds . . . [who] . . . sing in September their songs of the May-time." In "Bell-Birds" Kendall recalled the seasonal association of English poetry in which "May-time" is traditionally spring-time; in the "land down under" springtime is in September when "Grey winter hath gone, like a wearisome guest."[53] The contemporary Australian poet, now at home with his own tradition, takes his seasons for granted. He may be appreciative of Kendall's talent, but he thinks of him, if he thinks of him at all, as being meaningful only in historical terms.

VII *Slessor's View of His Predecessors*

Thus Slessor, himself an "historical figure," was distressed at
the attention paid Kendall in *The Oxford Book of Australasian
Verse*. That the editors in 1944 allocated over a dozen pages to
Kendall's poetry seemed to him excessive. In devoting this space
to Kendall, they had treated niggardly superior but less blatantly
"Australian" poets who had come after him. To Slessor, the
problem was that the editors had been influenced by "historical
or sentimental reasons, and not by the merciless and completely
unsentimental yardstick of pure poetry."[54] Slessor's complaint
in 1944 was justified, as it was fourteen years earlier when he
appealed for an anthologizing of Australian poetry on the basis
of "literary values" rather than for reasons of "museum-keep-
ing";[55] it was equally justified almost fourteen years later in
1957 when he objected to English critics who were comfortable
only with Australian poets who could be "pigeonholed as 'rough
diamonds,' 'cobbers,' 'bush poets,' 'colonial balladists,' etc."[56]

The problem, for Australian and English editors and critics
alike, was a strain of nationalism in Australian poetry that had
lingered too long, a nationalism that, in a muted way, lingers
today. Touched by nationalism, the early Australian poet had
been stimulated to struggle toward an indigenous poetry.
Touched by the poetry and the sentiment engendering it, the
critic and reader demanded that the poetry remain indigenous,
insisting on things "Australian" and on "local color" as marks
of distinction.

"One striking merit of Mr. Kendall's poetry," said the dean
of Australian critics in the 1860s "is that its coloring is strictly
local . . . and [the poet] has sought inspiration in the characters
and events of his country. He has chanted the savage melodies
of the aborigine—painted the suffering of the explorers—and
given a poetic interest to the life of the stockmen."[57] This was
the tone of early Australian criticism. It had been the same for
Harpur who had been praised by a reviewer in *Colonial Monthly*
for being "self-taught, self-relying, and self-contained," needing
no "old world models," but looking at Australian nature with a
"naked eye."[58]

It was the persistence of this point of view of what Australian
poetry should be that later was to encourage the mother country

to place the bust of a bush balladist, Adam Lindsay Gordon, a precursor to "Banjo" Paterson, in the Poets' Corner at Westminster Abbey. Not for his Byronic-inspired verse was the dashing English expatriate honored—the only poet from Australia ever to be so—but for his *Bush Ballads* and *Galloping Rhymes* (1870).

Perhaps Slessor was being excessive in his disenchantment a decade ago when he said that "the only poetry the English critic is prepared to accept from Australians is the kind for which Adam Lindsay Gordon received English commendation." And that "the English critic bitterly resents the intrusion of poetry which falls into what is regarded as the English preserve of sophistication or intellectual or cerebral poetry."[59] But it is apparent that when a place in "The Corner" had been found for a poet from Australia the poet was easily recognizable as an indigenous one.[60]

VIII   *Relations Between Old and New*

"Gone are the days of the poems of the gum-tree, the kookaburra, and the Stockrider," enthused *The Daily Mail* of Brisbane when Slessor's *Poetry in Australia 1923*, published by the Vision Press appeared in 1924.[61] In terms of the delightfully "different" poems included in the anthology, the enthusiasm was understandable. From co-editor Jack Lindsay's "Aphrodite" through Hugh McCrae's "Bacchanalia," to Slessor's "Thief of the Moon," the spirit was gay and fanciful, lyrical and delicate—quite un-bush-like. No balladist was represented nor any of that special breed of good men, "nationalists of the nineties," armed with an "Ode for Commonwealth Day" or some verse on "The Dominion of Australia."[62]

But *The Daily Mail* was overly optimistic. The kookaburra and gum-tree were hardy Australians and hardier still was the nationalistic sentiment in poetry that was to continue to give them life. Thirty years afterward in his autobiography, *The Roaring Twenties,* Jack Lindsay was to recall his departure in 1926 for England after the demise of the *Vision* magazine: "I left Ken [Slessor] . . . to fight . . . and turned my back on a problem which is still [in 1952] rendering Australian culture." And what was the problem? "A nationalism and popular philistinism that wanted nothing but loping narratives in verse, [in

effect], . . . a conflict between a national literature and a literature absorbing world culture."[63] Today, "consciousness of" rather
than "conflict between" is more accurate, and the phrase "still
rendering" seems exaggerated. But, by and large, in his remembering, Lindsay, the poet exiled by the problem, did indicate
its permanence and the nature of its change.

Yet the important point is not that kookaburras and gum-trees
and what they symbolized have endured, but that after Slessor
had done his work, poems about them changed and became better poems, and that poems with a whole new range of subject
matter, put together with a new craft, appeared to excite the
reader and make him more sophisticated and selective. Poetic
nationalism, which had created the beginning of an indigenous
poetry but had persisted to stifle its growth, had been significantly challenged. And this challenge, after Slessor, was sufficient to cause action and reaction, to stir up and bring a creative vitality to the whole of Australian poetry.

Two movements, the Jindyworobaks[64] in 1938 and the Angry
Penguins in the early forties, might be viewed today, in part, as
polar expressions of the response to the challenge. The Jindyworobaks, incited to search for a more national poetic image,
moved backward into the bush and into the depths of aboriginal
culture. "These my tribal grounds although my skin is white," was
their chant. On the other hand the Angry Penguins, inspired to
seek not a national but an individual, personal image," waddled at
the heels of the most pronounced kinds of modernism,"[65] and
went forward into surrealism and Freudian theories of associa-
tive thought. "Homunculus, hail! Yon deft epitome/Of Tambur-
laine and Twankydil's apt dwarf!" sang Ern Malley whose poems
were embraced by the Angry Penguins before they learned that
Ern and his poems were a hoax concocted by more conservative
poets who wished to discredit the Penguin movement.[66]

The Penguins and the Jindyworobaks were extreme responses,
hardly typical then or now of Australian poetry, and about
neither movement was Slessor particularly concerned. In his
view, to do as the Jindyworobaks seemed to advocate and
"return to the language and imagery of Australian black men . . .
would . . . be as reasonable as to suggest that an Australian
painter should restrict himself to carving kangaroos on the walls
of caves—or that, to lead a truly Australian life, we should take

up our abode in bark huts and paint our legs with clay." However, he would not condemn them if they "[would] keep their honesty and sincerity, and refuse to betray the faith in which English poets have worked, according to their own lights, since English poetry began."[67]

For the avant-garde Penguins, Slessor, the pioneer modernist, had little sympathy or interest and thought them "misguided." Yet how could the Penguins, "convinced that poetry had to be liberated from all poetic diction and conventional association,"[68] expect to find favor with a poet who, though he encouraged "experiments in anarchy" and sought freedom for his contemporaries, insisted that "the traditional grammar of rhyme, metre and formality, must be learnt by any poet as earnestly as the pianist learns his five-finger exercises"?[69] And how could they who "built up a monolith of obscure cult-ridden subjectivism"[70] earn support from a modernist who insisted on the concrete image which communicated to the ear, the mind, the heart and eye?[71] Slessor's voice, at once a liberating and moderating one, helped to enlist the poet on the side of poetry as against ideology. Whether a poem was a good poem became the primary consideration, not the poet's attitude toward the aboriginal or toward European estheticism. Henceforth, among the poets, if not always the critics, the *poetic* determinant was to prevail, easing even the last "conflict," that of the fifties, between a nationalist school which grew out of the unifying experiences of World War II, and an influential group of traditionally minded University poets.

IX *The Contemporary Position*

Today, the distinction between a "nationalist" poetry and an "international" one increasingly blurs. It is possible, of course, to identify poets who seem more conscious of the Australian experience and others who seem less so. Yet, more typical, is the poet who writes not only of the bush and Australian mythology, but also of urban problems and parking meters, of atomic scientists and current literary censorship. Increasingly more representative is the poet who, though recalling the "bora ring" of the aborigine and the bullock driver of the bush, will translate them above the local to a universal meaning. There are indigenous Australian echoes in contemporary Australian verse,

but there are also French echoes, of Mallarmé and Valéry, and
German ones of Rilke, and so on. And if the modern voices
of Eliot and Auden and Pound and Yeats are present, so are the
Augustan ones of Pope and Swift. Particularly in the satire and
beautifully controlled and lucid verse of Australia's greatest
practicing poet, A. D. Hope,[72] is the eighteenth century recalled
and brought up to date, serving not only Australians but men
everywhere.

The Australian contemporary poet today "turn[s] gladly
home."[73] Now comfortable with both his land and its traditions
and the older ones from which they grew, he moves with as-
surance to review his past, report his present, and predict his
future. If he still looks to some extent to England (and somewhat
to the United States) for critical approbation, he does so with
a sense of his own worth and with little if any of those past
feelings of inferiority which literary critic A. A. Phillips char-
acterized as the "cultural cringe." He is an Australian poet, and
he does not consider the fact of this either a "disability or a claim
to merit."[74] If there remain critics who occasionally still praise
a poet's work for containing no reference to wallabies (small
kangaroos), while others regard wallaby-less poems "as somewhat not quite Australian,"[75] they are not many and instances
of their critical myopia are rare. But rare as they are, the contemporary poet is impatient with them. "We do not want to be
valued for writing poems about wallabies," says the very fine
poet, Judith Wright, "or for soaring above wallabies to more
universal levels; we want to be valued for writing poems which
are good poems. . . . It is the poem we make that matters."[76]

"It is the poem we make that matters." Who today in Australia
would deny Miss Wright this point of view? Many would have,
thirty-five years before when Slessor first asked that the only
test of a good poem be its success "in transferring its beauty
without loss to the reader's mind." Realized now is much that
was hoped for in 1931 when "an interesting paper on 'Experiments in Modern English Poetry' was read by Mr. Kenneth
Slessor to members of the Australian English Association in the
Blue Room[77] [of the Sydney Hotel] on the evening of the 17th
September." At a time when Australian poetry was without
direction Kenneth Slessor helped point the way and poetry in
the "Land Down Under" has blossomed ever since.

CHAPTER 2

The Early Years: 1919-1926
Vision and Earth-Visitors

"Unlike anything else previously printed in Australia . . . the first quarterly worthy of the adjective 'literary' . . . will prove a delight to the many, . . . initiation to a few . . . and annoyance to undiscriminating prudes who will probably have it shut out of the libraries." This was the response of the Sydney press when the first issue of *Vision* magazine "written from the standpoint of the Dionysian intoxicated with life, and drunken with the glory of youth" appeared in May 1923.[1]

I *The Makers of* Vision

Our interest in the magazine is that the twenty-two-year-old Kenneth Slessor was one of its editors and that some of his early poems were to appear in its pages and in the *Vision* anthology, *Poetry in Australia 1923*,[2] and to reappear three years later with other poems in his first important collection, *Earth-Visitors*.[3] We are interested in *Vision* also because it grew out of and expressed a spirit of vitality and belief in beauty and imagination that served Slessor the man and the poet. That *Vision* also helped to create the spark for Slessor (and others) to lighten up Australian poetry—as its co-editor, Jack Lindsay would have it—does not seem overstated. Nor does the evaluation that *Vision* "gave Australian poetry a much needed stimulus in the twenties," and through Slessor and others, particularly FitzGerald, provided Australian poetry, almost for the first time, with examples of "vigour, vivid imagination, and traditional craftsmanship of high quality."[4]

It is possible that without Jack Lindsay's father, Norman, and his black-and-white drawings of bare-breasted mermaids and sly-staring satyrs, *Vision* might not have attracted as much attention. Lindsay, a versatile artist and writer, had long been

a controversial figure because of his provocative ideas about
sex, art, and beauty and his devotion to the voluptuous nude.
Giving the magazine its name, Norman Lindsay was also to be
the guru of the *Vision* movement, his son Jack its spokesman, and
Ken Slessor its most important poet. Yet if Lindsay's drawings
helped to bring the reader to *Vision*—and subsequent issues
enticed him further with naked nymphs and prancing fauns—the
appeal of the magazine's poetry and prose kept him there. Of
course not all of the poetry and less of the prose were uniformly
good, but some of it was, and all was vastly different from that
to which the reader had been accustomed.

That *Vision* was to be a vehicle in which the reader was to
ride in a direction almost opposite to any he had known, was
indicated from the outset. The magazine was covered by a
Norman Lindsay illustration of a long-haired Pan chasing a
butterfly and opened with a call from Jack Lindsay for poetry
and prose "that liberates the imagination by gaiety or fantasy."
Then came two songs by the delightful Hugh McCrae, Norman's old friend, and immediately after on page 7 Slessor's
"Thief of the Moon," decorated with a Lindsay drawing of a
kind of female faun bidding farewell to her mate astride a
winged horse. The sophisticated reader sensed what was hap-
pening and quickly responded. Caught up in the spirit and
ideals of *Vision*, the critic for the *Sydney Morning Herald*
warmed to the "exuberance and the joy of life" in the magazine,
and the reviewer for the *Sydney Daily Telegraph* discovered
in it new possibilities for cultural freedom: Australian writers
"who do not wish to conform to demands for local colour [now
have] a better chance to do original work."[5]

For the less sophisticated, *Vision*, being so different, may have
presented a problem. Certainly there were readers who had
ridden too long with "Clancy of the Overflow" or had listened
too long to the laughing kookaburra and his

> Ho, ho! ha, ha! with a glad refrain
>   which many mistake for scorn;
> But who find disdain in my joyous strain
>   was never a poet born
> ("The Kookaburra" by E. S. Emerson)

Not many poets had been born from such poetry; and a reader, nourished on it, on ballads and patriotic verse, might have had to learn how to delight in *Vision* and Slessor's poetry. Without the familiar wattle or waratah or whip, how was he to deal with that "Thief of the Moon."

> . . . thou robber of old delight,
> Thy charms have stolen the star-gold, quenched the moon—
> Cold, cold are the birds that, bubbling out of night
> Cried once to my ears their unremembered tune—
> Dark are those orchards, their leaves no longer shine,
> No orange's gold is globed like moonrise there—
> O thief of the earth's old loveliness, once mine,
> Why dost thou waste all beauty to make thee fair? (10)

If for some, the poetry at first did not make the *Vision* point, the prose did. "We would bring back the Goddess to Poetry, Music, and Art," said Jack Lindsay in his long essay on "Australian Poetry and Nationalism,"

and if we can sing new songs fragrant with this desire we shall have proved our youth and freedom as no chants about bullocks and droughts can prove it. . . . In Gaiety and Beauty the gods descend to earth, and those who build that bridge have done more for their countrymen than any patriotic balladmonger or realist can ever do.[6]

There was more involved in the *Vision* ethic than a call for gaiety and song and a distaste for the old nationalism in poetry. *Vision* was a turning away from death and depression lingering from the war years and a turning to a fresh impulse toward life. To classics student Jack Lindsay, such an impulse required "the Greek to come to life in Australia." How? "Not of course by merely writing hymns to the Olympians . . . but by a profound response to life, by the expression of lyric gaiety, by a passionate sensuality, by the endless search for the image of beauty, the immortal body of desire that is Aphrodite."[7] This was the only way, Lindsay believed, that "we may found a genuine Australian literature." For it was a shortsighted nationalism that could be proud only of verse about shearers and horses, "and measures the reality of a work by its local references."

If we wish to express an Australian spirit, let us make the spirit worth expressing by adding to it all the stimulus of sensuous and lyric imagery we can, by creating beauty so that the general consciousness may be further vitalized.[8]

There seems little question that much of the spirit that moved Jack Lindsay also moved the other contributors to *Vision*. Poet Hugh McCrae, in fact, had been a precursor of that spirit in the neglected *Satyrs and Sunlight* (1910). And all Visionites seem touched by the elder Norman's ideas proclaimed in *Creative Effort*[9] and elsewhere about artistic consciousness and the artist's responsibility to add beauty and power to human life. "Search for all that common minds reject as useless to the struggle for Existence," Lindsay assured, "and you will find all that serves life."

II   *Slessor and the* Vision *Group*

By temperament, more diffident and contemplative than the others, Slessor seems to have been less caught up in the "crusade." Although a confident reporter already owning a power with language and beginning to apply it to poetry, he had little of the surety of the Lindsays that he was one of a select group of *Übermenschen* who were to bring about a cultural renaissance. Slessor most certainly entered and absorbed in part, the Lindsayian world but he did so with a sense of detachment. Always stimulated by the Lindsays, particularly Norman, he seems to have taken from that world what he needed as a poet, and as a person. It is probable also that his distance was due in part to the fact that he had other commitments: he was already a full-time professional newspaperman, and he was also married to the lovely Noela, "slender and elegant with pretty ringlets."[10]

Yet Slessor appreciated that more than the pressure of time was involved, that *Vision* had a larger meaning for his co-editor, Jack Lindsay, than it did for him. "Of course, to Jack, *[Vision]* was more than a spare-time job," Slessor was to recall. "It was a full-time job and part of his need."

[The creed] was a very odd mixture of Nature and Greek mythology and all kinds of thundering pronouncements, and a lot of it I never agreed with. I did agree on point of dogma. I agreed very earnestly.

That was our insistence on the concrete image in art and our hatred of the abstract image. That has been my attitude to poetry, at least, ever since. I think that view in *Vision* is one that really provides the difference between what passes for poetry, and what is poetry. . . .[11]

This is good remembering. If part of the barrage of Visionite ideas missed a preoccupied Slessor, most certainly those concerned with the concrete image did not. The image was crucial to the young Slessor. Later he was to say that he was convinced that "the whole structure of English poetry . . . rests on the use of the image, the choice of the concrete when the abstract would be less racking to the creator, and certainly less searching in its revelations of his power or lack of power."[12]

III *The Influence of Norman Lindsay*

Norman Lindsay, in particular, in whose paintings, etchings, and sculpture, Slessor saw "a full art of the concrete and not the abstract,"[13] was especially meaningful. From the beginning, Slessor's inclinations seem to have been toward the materiality of the world and not its abstractions. Perhaps the requirements for the young reporter in the Roaring Twenties when he had to interview and describe for a not-too-intellectual reader everyone from "murderers to archbishops" reinforced his tendency toward the concrete and sensuously actual. Certainly, Norman Lindsay, by philosophy and example, did so.

Overly generous and usually precise in acknowledging influences, Slessor has not specifically indicated Lindsay's significance for his early verse. He has said, speaking at a meeting of the Commonwealth Literary Fund, that "My own debt to Norman Lindsay's perpetual power-house of stimulation and suggestion is obvious."[14] Less obvious is how much of the stimulation came from Lindsay the man and how much from his work. Both were impressive and both touched Slessor. "Altogether a devil or altogether a god," as Hugh McCrae would have him, Lindsay, to Slessor looking back, was also as close to a genius as "any other artist . . . Australia produced . . . an overflowing and inexhaustible spring of mental energy . . . creative fury . . . and almost universal craftsmanship."[15]

Lindsay did more for the young poet than simply stimulate, suggest, exhort, excite, and provide understanding. Slessor re-

members that "when Lindsay found a young poet's work which
he thought was vital, fresh and musical or gave promise of
development to come . . . many times he would quite spon-
taneously offer to wing the manuscript with drawings—and drawings by Norman Lindsay, even a tailpiece or a mere decoration,
could mean the difference between publication and oblivion."[16]

Slessor, ultimately, was not comfortable with a Lindsay illlus-
tration or any illustration to his poetry. A believer in the intrinsic
integrity and self-containment of a poem, it seemed "a contradic-
tion that a poem in which time is fluid should be fixed to an
instant by the illustration of a few of its lines." Nor should the
imagination, "which may be given infinity when released by a
poem, be limited by the finite dimensions of a drawing. The
Forest of Arden of the mind's eye is obviously far superior to
the Forest of Arden supplied by the most talented scene-
painter."[17] Norman Lindsay agreed with these principles, but was
willing to sacrifice them, as was Slessor, to get poetry published.
The twenties were difficult times for poetry in Australia.

It is probable that Norman Lindsay also served the young
Slessor as an example of the hard-working artist. For the burgeoning poet this was important. Backboned by the demands of
his newspaper work, Slessor's attitude toward his spare-time
poetry writing seems from the outset to have been scrupulously
professional. Yet the excitement, excessiveness, and goodfellow-
ship of Sydney's poetic circles could be diverting, even for the
detached and committed Slessor. A supportive to his own sense
of work was meaningful at the time. Jack Lindsay and Hugh
McCrae, delightful companions though they were, could not
provide this; only Norman could. Already settled in rural Springwood, away from the distractions of Sydney, Lindsay in labor
was the prototype of the dedicated craftsman who stayed with
his work and wrought out splendid products. Slessor marveled at
the genius in "every stroke of his brush or pen or etching-needle,
on the painted canvas, the written page or the copper sheet."[18]
No poet subsequently was to work harder than Slessor to perfect his art, "always experimenting, always obsessed with poetry
as a craft." A "verbal dandy,"[19] through the *Vision* days, Slessor
the poet and person, was to mature through the thirties and
emerge after *Five Bells* (1939) as a master of poetic form and
language, a poet of power, delicacy, and depth.

A more palpable Lindsayian influence may be suggested by Professor R. G. Howarth's analysis that finds Slessor's earlier verse, written between 1919 and 1926 and appearing in *Vision* Magazine (1924)[20] and the volume *Earth-Visitors* (1926) as appealing primarily to the "eye, then to ear—little to mind." Slessor's ultimate grasp of the image was to be a total one, involving an appeal to all the senses, and Professor Howarth is both correct and felicitous of expression in assigning to Slessor's last poems, written between 1933 and 1939 and appearing first in *Five Bells* (1939), and to the single "Beach Burial" (1942), a "complex enticement of ear, mind, heart, and eye."[21]

Yet Slessor, student of Tennyson, had said that from the earliest time he was "always more concerned with the aural effect rather than the pictorial sense."[22] What then is the reason for the stronger visual appeal in the earlier verse? Might it not be an influence of Lindsay the *painter* whose representational art depicted so vividly "the full art of the concrete"? For Howarth is correct again in seeing that Slessor's verse of the middle period, written from 1927 to 1932 and published in *Cuckooz Contrey* (1932) (by which time he had grown away from Lindsay), "evinces a reduction of the visual element [and] an increase of the aural"[23]—an emphasis which is truer to Slessor who sought, like Tennyson, to write "music in words."[24]

Certainly the visual element seems strongest in the early poems. Vivid are those "Plump cherubim with blown cheeks" and those strange riders "Cloaked in dark furs, with faces grave and sweet." No less so are "Those friends of Lao-Tzu, those wise old men/Dozing all day in lemon-silken robes./With tomes of beaten jade spread knee to knee."[25] One easily remembers in the mind's eye not only the persona but the things of Slessor's early world:

> Those frescoes cut with curious flowers,
> In verdigris and lilac-reds
>
> .   .   .   .
>
>
> And fire-fish in the topaz fount
> With red fins blown like water-plants,
> And green cornelian tortoise-rows . . . [26]

Or the mist of "water breathing in the air," or the sun that
"comes up in a golden stain, floats like a glassy sea-fruit . . .
[and] diamonds the wind-cocks, makes glitter the crusted
spikes."[27] And one sees again and quotes without effort lines
about "waterspouts of lace and bubbling rings"[28] and "The spires
of Paris, pricked in an iron spume," and:

> Hamburg—those roofs of tulip-red, those floating trees,
>   Those black masts clotting the air, and swart cigars,
> And puffed old bankers panting along the quays,
>   And Uncle Solomon shouting amongst the spars,
> And Uncle Solomon's cargoes, coffee and cheese,
>   And Uncle Solomon's face, like a copper moon,
> And Uncle Solomon's daughter, and the stars, the stars.[29]

Looking at Slessor's early poems of *Vision* and *Earth-Visitors*,
it is difficult to disentangle one from the other the influence of
the man Lindsay and Lindsay the artist and the realities of his
art. Slessor dedicates poems to both and the poems reflect his
dual commitment, often simultaneously. For example, it is to
Lindsay's work, "To the etchings of Norman Lindsay" that
Slessor dedicates his poem, "Realities" which appears in *Earth-
Visitors*:

> Now the statues lean over each to each, and sing,
> Gravely in warm plaster turning; the hedges are dark.
> The trees come suddenly to flower with moonlight,
> The water-gardens to glassy fire, and the night, the night,
> Breaks in a rain of stars. O, now the statues wake. . . . (32)

What are the "realities" here? They are first the etched crea-
tions of Lindsay's artistic imagination, images of beauty. They
are then Slessor's response to the etchings—the poem, his own
expression of beauty, his "Realities." Thus beauty begets beauty.
In that the images of beauty, the etchings and the poem, are
called "realities," they represent a point of view about their
significance—a Lindsayian point of view. And to reinforce his
embracement of the idea that beauty constitutes the "realities,"
the only worthwhile realities of life, and that beauty is alive
for him, Slessor gives actual life to the etching in his poem, and
soon: "Venus with Venus is walking in a misty grove,/Their

mouths breathless with great lies of Jove,/ . . . [and] Flowers turn to faces; faces like small gold panes,/Are bodied with a mist of limbs—no dark remains."

But Slessor does even more to underline the point that for him the world of imagination and images of beauty in Lindsay's etchings (and, by inference, in Slessor's poem dedicated to them) *are* the "Realities":

> And I, who have climbed in these unrooted boughs
> Behind the world, find substance there and flesh,
> Thoughts more infrangible than windly vows,
> Love that's more bodily, and kisses longer,
> And Cythera lovelier, and the girls of moonlight stronger
> Than all earth's ladies, webbed in their bony mesh.

IV *Imagination Versus Reality*

Yet more than the world of imagination and the etchings are involved in Slessor's response. For if Slessor had "climbed in these unrooted boughs/Behind the world," he had also climbed in *rooted* boughs *in* the world—Lindsay's actual, physical world— the gardens surrounding his home. "For more than forty years (now fifty)," Slessor tells us in a Commonwealth Literary Fund Lecture, "Norman Lindsay has rarely stirred from his home in the bush to the north of Springwood, where he lives with monk-like abstemiousness in an old stone house, surrounded by the gardens, pools, and statues which he has made himself."[30] Slessor knows these gardens, pools, and statues well, and could recall, as Norman's son Jack does, a trip out from Sydney to Springwood and "a stroll about the gardens among the cypresses and the life-like statues of satyrs and nymphs-silver-thighed statues in concrete, which has to be finished in a day" or possibly a swim in "the bathing pool built half down a gully, with a concrete nymph shading her unimaginable face as she peers into the pale green water rippling at a falling gum seed."[31]

A sense of this "place" where Norman Lindsay lives is part of Slessor's response in "Realities" and is present in several of his early poems. It is discovered, almost in passing, in "Earth-Visitors" as one of the few places where the Goddess of beauty, Venus, feels free to visit: "When darkness has arched his hands over the bush/And Springwood steams with dew, . . " (1). And

it is revealed in fuller measure in Slessor's longest *Vision* poem,
"The Man of Sentiment"[32] with lines suggestive at once of a
Lindsay etching and of the gardens at Springwood itself. The
poem, cast in dramatic form, opens in a walled garden at York
in which the writer Laurence Sterne and Catherine de Fromantel,
"a girl who sings at Ranelagh . . . pause at a path which runs
between hedges and cypress trees." Catherine is reluctant to
proceed because "such paths have led to dangerous lands before,/And many a maid's marched less than fifty steps/To-day
no maiden. . . ." But Laurence says:

> Nay, 'tis no Devil's walk,
> It leads to what? Some leaden Child with lips
> Blown open, spouting fountain-dew on birds
> That drowsily dive the pool . . . some secret Lawn
> Tight locked away in mazes and trod by none
> Save one old crazy Gardener . . . aye, 'tis prick'd
> In curious inks on charts of old, I'll vow. . . .(16)

The atmosphere of the walled garden, its paths and hedges,
the statue of the "leaden Child with lips/Blown open, spouting
fountain-dew on birds/"—all this seems familiar, echoing from
the real and the fanciful. The "old crazy Gardener," custodian
of the mystery, had been seen before in life, and in the etchings
celebrated in the poem, "Realities"; he is "the old Gardener . . .
grown old with raking [who] . . . hears . . . Mercury whispering
to some . . . graven Boys." And the cypresses in the garden of
Springwood among which Slessor strolled, are not unlike those
at York toward which Laurence urges Catherine: "Come . . .
seven steps . . . I'll swear to coax no more . . ./As far as the
Cypress . . . not a bee's foot further. . . ./As far as the
Cypress. . . ."

If it is difficult to disentangle the influence on Slessor's early
verse of Lindsay's actual gardens from the art relating to them,
it is no less difficult to separate these influences from the man
in the garden who "with his piercing, sky blue eyes, speaks as
from the Apollonian tripod . . . in [a] sweeping flood . . . of
eloquent idealism" or who "reads with abrupt boyish shouts
of laughter."[33] Lindsay the man, the believer in life, "*la sacre
vie*,"[34] touched the young Slessor.

It is: "To N. L." that the developing poet dedicates the title poem of his first important collection, *Earth-Visitors*. Originally the seventh poem in order in the volume that appeared in 1926, Slessor was to make it the first and introductory poem when he put together his major collection, *One Hundred Poems* (1944), and keep it in this exalted position with the original dedication throughout the more than half-dozen reprints which have been published through 1969-70 under the title *Poems.*[35] In effect, the older Slessor, looking back over a quarter of a century, made "Earth-Visitors" his set-piece, the point from which he moved toward maturity as a person and poet.

"Earth-Visitors" is not only dedicated *to* Norman Lindsay, it is, in part, *about* him and his place, Springwood. He may be simply imagined as one of the gods, "strange riders" who "came gusting down to earth" in legendary times, or specifically mentioned as that one who is able to welcome Venus:

> When darkness has arched his hands over the bush
> And Springwood steams with dew, and the stars look down
> On that one lonely chamber . . . [where Lindsay works in
>   behalf of beauty]
> She is there suddenly, lit by no torch or moon,
> But by the shining of her naked body.
> Her breasts are berries broken in snow; her hair
> Blows in a gold rain over and over them.
> She flings her kisses like warm guineas of love,
> And when she walks, the stars walk with her above.
> She knocks. The door swings open, shuts again.
> "Your name, child?"
> A thousand birds cry "Venus!" (2)

Whether or not Slessor dedicated a poem to the man Lindsay or to his art, as he does specifically in "Earth-Visitors" and "Realities," or if he does not, as in "The Man of Sentiment" and "Thieves Kitchen," something of Lindsay is usually present. No Lindsayite would have difficulty, for example, in seeing the resemblance between the picturesque vagabonds and rogues depicted by Lindsay and those who appear in "Thieves." Published in the second, (August) issue of *Vision*, Slessor's poem, vital and gay as Lindsay's art, urges life:

> Leap, leap, fair vagabonds, your lives are short . . .
> Dance firelit in your cauldron-fumes, O thieves,
> Ram full your bellies with spiced food, gulp deep
> Those goblets of thick ale—yea, feast and sport,
> Ye Cyprian maids—lie with great, drunken rogues,
> Jump by the fire—soon, soon your flesh must crawl
>   And Tyburn flap with birds, long-necked and swart! (25)

That Slessor "ventured into the Lindsay world" and drew "sustenance"[36] from it, as Jack Lindsay suggests in his autobiography, *The Roaring Twenties,* is as obvious as Slessor's expressed debt to Norman Lindsay's "perpetual powerhouse of ideas and stimulations." Yet, looking back, neither sees the young Slessor as being fully committed to this world, to being truly "caught up" in its ideas and excitement. Slessor, as indicated, says he "never agreed with" a lot of its "thundering pronouncements" and its "very odd mixture of nature and Greek mythology." And Jack Lindsay recalls that "Ken," his co-editor, "did not at any time share our fanatical universe . . . [though] in his own way [he] drew a certain sustenance from our ideas and enthusiasms."[37]

V *Limitations of the Lindsayian World*

With Slessor's poetry of the time in hand, the picture that emerges from these recollections and others, is that of a young poet subject to influence, particularly from a forceful personality, but more often than not, choosing that which he wishes to be influenced by. (Of course we are helped here by our knowledge of Slessor's subsequent poetic and psychological development.) There is a deliberateness about the young Slessor, a sensed need for emotionality, but a restraint and abiding consciousness that would filter and control it. He is, from the beginning, his own man thinking his own thoughts, wanting to become involved with others, but not too much so, somewhat fearful, as Jack Lindsay recalls, "that he would never be able to liberate all his powers with the daily grind of reporting,"[38] but, again, not too much so. He is tactful, courteous, and objective, aware of himself, certainly, but careful to place that self in balance and perspective (he will struggle to relate that self to his poetry).

Fastidious in manner and dress, devoted to his job as a journalist and to a wife, and somewhat inclined to prick romantic illusion, Slessor nevertheless ventured into the very different and unconventional Lindsay world. He entered this world because he had no other and needed one to evoke and direct his poetry. That the world to work with began with himself and moved outward, may have been apparent to the young person but seems less so to the young poet. In these early years, poetry does not seem central to his being: he is not driven from within, but seeks external stimuli on which to exercise his imagination and practice his craft. The *Vision* Lindsay world, devoted to gaiety and fantasy and fun in the flesh, and to times and places and figures away from the familiar and pedestrian, provided something of that which he sought; possibly also something of that which he actually needed.

This is not to suggest that the young Slessor brought little to that world; as indicated he was already his own man, thinking his own thoughts and devoted to professionalism in his work and his art. Certainly Slessor brought his sharp intelligence, a background of wide reading, his charm, a wonderful wit, a "powerfully accurate eye," and the beginnings of a control over language that no Australian had had before and none has had since. These were important resources, sufficient to breathe life into a movement that, for all its declaration and dedication to life, now seems lifeless, that for all its devotion to gaiety now seems sad.

Yet, for all of Slessor's ability to infuse some of his early poetry with a sense of life and palpable presence, there is about it something of the artificial and the forced. We might, of course, blame this, in part, on the subject matter and settings suggested by the Lindsays: the Greeks, the gods, the gay rogues, and the "good roaring pistol-boys." Or, possibly, assign fault to those encouraged flights of imagination in pursuit of beauty which sent Slessor to travel with "Marco Polo," to sit with the "Taoist," or to dream with "Heine in Paris."

The strange and exotic, however, presented no problem for Slessor; he had, indeed, a penchant for them. Where some of the poems floundered—and even when they do they are lovely to read—is their emotionality or lack of it. Simply put, the poet does not seem to be emotionally involved with his poem—and this disturbs. That he is not, comes not from want of trying; in fact, it may well be that just because he tries so hard to be emotionally connected that the honesty of his feelings is suspected and the shallowness revealed. Certainly, to some extent, the problem probably has to do with Slessor's loyalty to the *vital* Lindsays and their game of gaiety, a gaiety with which he cannot fully identify. Having ventured into the Lindsays' world, he would play their game; it was his game too, now, and he *was* touched by it. And he would play the game well, for that was the only way to play it—if you would perfect your art— and it was for that purpose and for publication that he had entered the world.

But *playing* in the world was not the same as truly *believing* in it. It is this lack of belief that ultimately dilutes the reality of his early poetry, even in such a set-piece poem as "Earth-Visitors," his fantasy about the descent on a country town of a wenching band of pagan deities. The poet who, it may be recalled, later in the poem has Venus visit Lindsay, introduces his "Earth-Visitors" with a sharp vividness that appeals at once to the eye, and then to the ear:

> Post-boys would run, lanterns hang frostily, horses fume,
> The strangers wake the Inn. Men, staring outside
> Past watery glass, thick panes, could watch them eat,
> Dyed with gold vapours in the candleflame,
> Clapping their gloves, and stuck with crusted stones,
> Their garments foreign, their talk a strange tongue, . . . (1)

On one level, that of the life of man, this is a poem of nonsense, of make-believe. On another, as an expression of beauty created by imagination, the poem has a reality of its own which we can relate to. Slessor's power with language has wrought an illusion of life which almost completely involves us—but not quite. For we will not enter into the life of the poem unless accompanied by the poet—and the poet only *presents* the poem, he is not present in it.

This is Slessor's problem in several of his early poems. Loyal though he is to the idea of gaiety and exuberance, he cannot feel it. And though he may urge, for example, his "fair vaga-bonds" of "Thieves Kitchen" to "leap, leap," for their "lives are short" and to greet with a toast his "Good roistering easy maids, blown cock-a-hoop/On floods of tavern-steam," he seems unable to leap with them or to truly drink with his maids. Slessor seems essentially apart from his poem and is left posturing upon it. The world of the mind that he creates is only of the mind, not of the heart, and though he is able to pulsate it with his verbal facility, the world is finally a kind of cardboard world, pressed into being.

VI   *Movement toward "First-Hand Experience"*

Slessor seems to explain, if not specifically his lack of personal involvement in the early poetry, at least some of its artificial or second-hand quality—second-hand, in the sense of its seeming once removed from reality. In a radio interview with John Thompson, with whom he had edited the *Penguin Book of Modern Australian Verse* (1958), Slessor said that "the young writer writes from second-hand experience" because he doesn't have "very much experience—first-hand experience—from which to draw." Slessor's comment was in reply to Thompson's question as to why Slessor's early poetry had been full of exotic things. "You get mentions," Thompson had said:

springing from, say, Dürer, and then the god Pan, and the names of Rubens, Marco Polo, Heine—I think there's "Heine in Paris"—and Spain comes into it. I think the early work *has* got a strong exotic element in it, don't you?

Slessor agreed that it did, primarily because young writers "get their experiences second-hand, vicariously, from what they read."

Mine came mostly from what I read and the people that you mention, Heine and the Chinese, and Sterne and other writers of that kind, were the writers at that time who obsessed me. Therefore I was writing about *their* experiences and not *mine*. Later, when one grows older and obtains the sweets and the sours of existence, and has the first-hand experience of life, it's no longer necessary to draw from the experiences of reading.[39]

All this seems true, particularly when viewed from a distance of forty years after the days of *Vision* and *Earth-Visitors*. And given Thompson's specific questions and the interview situation, it is perhaps as inclusive an answer as Slessor could offer. Surely, though, Slessor would allow room for his own expressed "debt to Norman Lindsay's perpetual power-house of stimulation and suggestion" and the relationship of this debt to his readings of the time and to the writers who "obsessed" him.

Yet, apart from the understandable omission of Lindsay's influence on reading matter, there is a slightly disingenuous note in Slessor's answer, though it is probably less a conscious one and simply a casual embrace of a cliché. It has to do with Slessor's remarks about how, when the writer grows older and obtains "the sweets and the sours of existence," he no longer has to draw experiences from reading. This is all well and good and generally true, but less relevant in Slessor's case. Kenneth Slessor, the young writer we are discussing, was, at the time to which the older Slessor refers, no isolated poet living in an attic, simply reading books and writing poetry, and untouched by life's experience. Nor was he a kind of acolyte, as the late H. M. Green, Australia's distinguished literary historian would have it, working with Hugh McCrae, "in the studio of a common master [Lindsay] . . . sharing, though in different degrees, the master's enthusiasms . . . and developing his attitude in directions each of his own."[40] Even before Norman's son, Jack, had met him to begin the friendship which was to culminate in the publication of *Vision* magazine in the late spring of 1923, Slessor was a fairly sophisticated writer with his own ideas and a strong sense of himself, who was participating actively in the world. Jack recalls, for example, that before being introduced personally to Slessor (to be "charmed" by him), he had been "prejudiced against [him] through an article of his I had read in the news-paper . . . which was meant . . . to pinprick romantic illusions, but for me . . . upheld philistine positions."[41]

The point is that Slessor, at the time, was already a professional newspaperman who did know something of "the sweets and the sours of existence," who, in his own words in the same interview with Thompson, had been out in life, working among the people and interviewing everyone "from murderers to archbishops." And, if, as he said, he was simply using the "second-hand" experiences of others and not his own, of "writing about *their* experiences and not *mine*," it was not because he wasn't having "first-hand" experiences and living an emotional and involved life, it was because he wasn't seeing their relationship to his poetry. Poetry was still not central to his life experience, but something outside and separate from it. Poetry still belonged to a different, more remote, more exotic, possibly Lindsayian world. Slessor, less personally and more poetically committed, entered that world to make use of it, and responded to its content primarily in terms of the craft needed to present it artistically.

No one would question that the young Slessor made large use of the Lindsayian world, and that much of his early verse shows evidence that he knew well its inhabitants, their lives, feelings, and ideas. All ten poems[42] which he contributed to the four issues of *Vision* magazine reflect in varying degrees this familiarity, whether they deal with his "wenches, like fire-birds blown to flight" to whom he bids "Good-night!" or with his wait at "The Embarkation for Cythera" where "in the warm lake/There foam a thousand water-girls, blown deep/With rings of silver and bubbles like racing moons." And Lindsayites, in turn, would find harmonious the spirit at "Adventure Bay," port of drowned lovers, where mermaids ride "by waterspouts of lace and bubbling rings," or behind "The Mask" and Norman Lindsay's illustrations for it of a bare-breasted mermaid with flowing hair reaching for a flying bird.

Much the same can be said of Slessor's half-dozen poems not previously published in the magazine but which, with eight of the *Vision* poems, made up the anthology, *Poetry in Australia 1923*,[43] published by the Vision Press, with a preface by Norman Lindsay. The decorative "Pan at Lane Cove" with its gate beside which great fungi steam, "scaly with poison, bright with flame," and its garden and lonely faun over which "cold stars are bubbling round the moon" (4) echo and re-echo from the Lindsayian world, as do the wenches in "The Ghost":

> Wenches with tousled silk,
> Mouths warm and bubble eyes,
> Tumble those beds of milk
>   Under carved canopies.... (27)

So do, and somewhat monotonously the "Nights long forgotten, moons too dark to find,/Or stars too cold" in the "Man-

groves" (10) and the "perpetual trysting with the sombre moon"
of "Incongruity."[44] And the poet's surrender "to those Venus-
bergs, thy breasts," in the poem "A Surrender" (15) recall
simultaneously both a Lindsay illustration and a McCrae paean
to physicality and Slessor's own poem "Rubens' Innocents" from
the very first issue of *Vision*.

About "Nuremberg," the sixth anthology poem, more interesting things might be said. Here, happily, is one of those occasions,
too rare in this period, that Slessor moves away from the excessive lushness and loudness and emotional emptiness that
typifies his response to the Lindsayian experience. Here he is
restrained, deliberate, and, with a touch remarkably deft for
one so young, he carefully creates a mood which seems to come
finally from himself:

> So quiet it was in that high, sun-steeped room,
> So warm and still, that sometimes with the light
> Through the great windows, bright with bottle-panes,
> There'd float a chime from clock-jacks out of sight,
>   Clapping iron mallets on green copper gongs.
>
> But only in blown music from the town's
> Quaint horologe could Time intrude . . . you'd say
> Clocks had been bolted out, the flux of years
> Defied, and that high chamber sealed away
>   From earthly change by some old alchemist.
>
> And, oh, those thousand towers of Nuremberg
> Flowering like leaden trees outside the panes:
>   Those gabled roofs with smoking cowls and those
> Encrusted spires of stone, those golden vanes
>   On shining housetops paved with scarlet tiles! (3)

Wanting in the poem, as in most of the early *Vision* verse,
is an appeal to the mind; one wants more than simply an evoca-
tion of mood, beautifully rendered and honest though it is. Yet,
here, too, despite its absence of real intellectual content, the
poem offers a precursor of Slessor's later speculations on the
subject of time and its relationship to the human condition, a
subject that is to permeate much of his more significant poetry
in the middle and last periods. "Nuremberg" is meaningful also

in that it demonstrates aspects of Slessor's early strength in learning how to control language and curb an inclination toward verbal display possibly encouraged by the excesses he thought demanded of him by the Visionites.

VII   *The Poetry of* Earth-Visitors

All fourteen poems from the *Vision* anthology, *Poetry in Australia 1923*, were included with 21 others to make up *Earth-Visitors* (1926), Slessor's major publication of this first period. This is not to suggest that the *Vision* period poems were written before those appearing in *Earth-Visitors*. Slessor inclusively covers the writing of all 35 poems with the years 1919 to 1926;[45] that is, with the years immediately preceding the founding and publishing of *Vision* and ending with the publication of *Earth-Visitors*. Nor should we, looking at these years and relating them to specific poems, too casually refer to a poem as being "pre-Lindsayan" and one being not. There are blatant Lindsayan poems written early in the period before, biographically, Slessor became involved with the Lindsays. "Pan at Lane Cove" might be cited as one such poem. And there are muted Lindsayan poems, demonstrating other visions and possibilities, as "Nuremberg," written later in the period *after* Slessor had entered the Lindsayian world. The point is that for a number of years and in a variety of ways, directly and indirectly, Slessor's verse seems to have been subject to a Lindsayian influence. Yet, simultaneously, to a large extent, Slessor seems to have chosen the nature of that influence. Of course the young poet, in part, was caught up, but the young poet was able also to control to a considerable degree *how* he was caught. Thus, if most of the poems in *Earth-Visitors* reflect some aspect of the Lindsay-Vision ethos, so too is present a consciousness and concern that seems primarily Slessorian. This is particularly true of the poems not published previously in either *Vision* magazine or the *Vision* anthology. Yet reading these "new"[46] poems together with those collected from the *Vision* publications, we discover in the latter more of Slessor than noted before.

Slessor opens *Earth-Visitors* not with the title poem, dedicated "To N. L.," but with "Winter Dawn." Whether or not this is a poem written before "Earth-Visitors" and other poems of gaiety and fantasy is not known, but it is a poem different from those we have read. It is not of legendary times when pagan gods came "gusting down" to visit the earth, nor is it of nymphs or rogues of the Renaissance. The poem is of *now,* and the setting, "Winter Dawn" rising in Sydney. Here, as in "Nuremberg," we hear, for the most part, a restrained voice, deliberate and somber. And the voice, as it looks over the city and the lives of men, is moved by an inner vision that truly belongs to the poet:

> At five I wake, rise, rub on the smoking pane
> A port to see—water breathing in the air,
> Boughs broken. The sun comes up in a golden stain,
> Floats like a glassy sea-fruit. There is mist everywhere,
> White and humid, and the Harbour is like plated stone,
> Dull flakes of ice. One light drips out alone,
> One bead of winter-red, smouldering in the steam,
> Quietly over the roof-tops—another window
> Touched with a crystal fire in the sun's gullies,
> One lonely star of the morning, where no stars gleam,
>
> Far away on the rim of this great misty cup,
> The sun gilds the dead suburbs as he rises up,
> Diamonds the wind-cocks, makes glitter the crusted spikes
> On moss-drowned gables. Now the tiles drip scarlet-wet,
> Swim like birds' paving-stones, and sunlight strikes
> Their watery mirrors with a moister rivulet,
> Acid and cold. Here lie those mummied Kings,
> Men sleeping in houses, embalmed in stony coffins,
> Till the Last Trumpet calls their galleries up,
> And the suburbs rise with distant murmurings.
>
> O buried dolls, O men sleeping invisible there,
> I stare above your mounds of stone, lean down,
> Marooned and lonely in this bitter air,
> And in one moment deny your frozen town,
> Renounce your bodies—earth falls in clouds away,
> Stones lose their meaning, substance is lost in clay,
> Roofs fade, and that small smoking forgotten heap,
> The city, dissolves to a shell of bricks and paper,
> Empty, without purpose, a thing not comprehended,
> A broken tomb, where ghosts unknown sleep. (14)

Technically, "Winter Dawn" seems what it is: an early poem of an accomplished young poet learning his craft. The poem is strong and successful in introducing and building an image and evoking a mood; it is less so in sustaining them. The poem's voice, mostly clear and in control of setting the scene, as in the first two stanzas, is self-conscious and excessive in emotion in interpreting it, as in the third. And, if generally the poem's rhyme scheme serves the poet, sometimes, as in the couplet opening the second stanza, it fails him—though even here, some of the jar disappears if we move quickly, as the poet wishes us to, to the third line: "Diamonds the wind-cocks. . . ."

In his analysis of "Winter Dawn," the Australian poet-critic Max Harris also sees "a conflict in the poem between the kind of descriptive scene being essayed and the technical means adopted by the poet." By "technical means," Harris refers specifically to Slessor's language, "the adjectival heaping-up" that "creates a mood more of romantic sensualism" than the atmosphere sought by the poet, one that is "cold, crisp, and crystal-like."[47] The point of "conflict" is a useful one, though overstated for this particular poem. There is also merit in Harris's belief that the conflict in "Winter Dawn" is part of a larger problem of the young poet to locate a language suitable to his poetic temperament, a temperament which Harris sees as being "essentially elegiac and haunted by memories of the tragic and bitter."[48] These are important considerations, but our interest at this juncture is less in the poem's craft and more in the poet's concern and emotionality; these provide the link to the later great poet.

The somber "I" of "Winter Dawn," who wakes "at five" and looks out over the city to see the "buried dolls" of men, is the poet engagé, the poet involved in his poem and using it to express his deep feelings and concern. It is a far different "I" and one truer to itself, than the gay "I" who "stems the tide" at "Adventure Bay" or teases the "easy maids" of the "Thieves Kitchen." For already is heard the note that is to sound in the later poems, the note of disillusionment with contemporary life and all that men would make of it. And already is felt the first frustration about man's transitoriness and life's mystery and absurdity. A phrase, in fact, from the final and fourth stanza, "O Sun that kills with life," sends forth almost existential echoes to blend with reverberations from Camus's lucid despair: "Everything that exalts life increases at the same time its absurdity."

Other poems in *Earth-Visitors* sustain this note, and still others broaden it. In "Marco Polo" Slessor at first delights in memories of a bygone life "Where Kublai's five-clawed dragons glowed/ Like painted wyverns" and where he

> . . . saw tall gilded Tartars pass
> Behind their marble balustrades,
> With maces made of beaten brass
> And turquoise-hafted sabre-blades.

But he delights too much, and the present pales in comparison, and all the "glittering visual imagery [of the poem] is pinched to a bitter end"[49] in the last couplet: "I'm sick of modern men. I wish/You still were living, Kublai Khan!" (8)

There is even a kind of bitter-sweet sadness in the beginning of "Heine in Paris" as the old man, left alone, "Knees hugged in bed, the drug purring in his brain," remembers the days of his youth and the bright mad girls, now "all gone, or paunched in marriage, or crushed in graves." But at the end only the bitterness remains and a sense of desolation and futility envelops him as his thoughts linger over his own life and that of other men. What meaning has life? What value man's efforts? Life goes on, but men die, and all is for naught: all wrong, all wasted. "What now was left of all the passion he'd spilled,/The fire he'd struck?" He is contemptuous of men's "fighting and coupling" and "ravening," their "warring, but nothing gained," their "babbling to silent Christs; climbing to heavens of the brain." For men ultimately are meaningless:

> Men crumbled, man lived on. In that animal's face
> 'Twas but a squirt aimed at the moon, to fling contempt.
> Meyerbeer, Borne, and Klopstock vanished, but in their place
> New Klopstocks, Meyerbeers blown again, and
> Bornes undreamt,
> Sprang up like fungi . . .
>
> .   .   .   .
>
> Heine looked out, and gazed at the world below,
> Thick with old chemicals, breaking far out of sight
> With ageless tides of man—ah, granite flow,
> Eternal, changeless flux of humanity,
> Undying darkness and light!

Not treading those floods could save him—not striking stone,
    Not damming the world could serve—only to fly,
Careless of men and their shouting—untouched—alone—
    Snatched by his own gods from a falling sky,
And singing his own way—clutching his own, his own,
    Blind to the world—yes, that was the road of Heine—
Up to the sun, solitary, a speck in the ether—

"Ha, now, Christ Jesus and Jehovah, I choose to die!" (12-13)

"I choose to die"—a far different cry from that emitted by the life-worshipping Lindsayites. Indeed, from the outset, they must have wondered at the strange promptings that had forced their young companion in gaiety to write about the embittered and empty old age of Heine rather than his gay and productive youth. Had not *Vision* been dedicated to the "younger generation" and to a condition of mind that was vital, hopeful, and ascending? Through what glass, darkly, had their friend peered, and what had been his vision, unseen by them? Slessor's vision was of the stars and the space beyond, it was beyond their earth and the flesh of it.

For the reader of the *Earth-Visitors* volume, the gay poem, "Adventure Bay," which immediately follows "Heine in Paris," relieves some of the grim echoes of the poet. In turn, "Bay's" spirit of fancy is sustained and heightened by the opening stanza of "Stars":

"These are the floating berries of the night,
    They drop their harvest in dark alleys down,
    Softly far down on groves of Venus, or on a little town
Forgotten at the world's edge—and O, their light
Unlocks all closed things, eyes and mouths, and drifts
    Quietly over kisses in a golden rain,
Drowning their flight, till suddenly the Cyprian lifts
    Her small, white face to the moon, then hides again.

.   .   .   .

"Should the girl's eyes be lit with swimming fire,
    O do not kiss it away, it is a star, a star! . . ."

Then, suddenly, almost without warning, except for a dropped quotation mark and a culminating line indicating that all this loveliness was but the cry of "the passionate poet to his great, romantic guitar," the reader is engulfed by a flood of horror: an empty black universe without God or design, a universe in which man is alone and without meaning:

> But I was beating off the stars, gazing, not rhyming.
>   I saw the bottomless, black cups of space
> Between their clusters and the planets climbing
>   Dizzily in sick airs, and desired to hide my face.
> But I could not escape those tunnels of nothingness,
>   The cracks in the spinning Cross, nor hold my brain
> From rushing for ever down that terrible lane,
>   Infinity's trap-door, eternal and merciless. (26)

Looking back from Slessor's later poetry, "Stars" seems a pivotal poem that points to "Gulliver" of the middle period, as "Gulliver" was to point to "Five Bells" of the last. In "Stars" Slessor has not yet discovered, as he was to in "Gulliver," the "most precise and eloquent image of the plight of modern man that Australian poetry is ever likely to produce."[50] Yet the image in "Stars" is of sufficient delineation and intensity that, together with those seen in "Heine in Paris," "Winter Dawn," and other *Earth-Visitors* poems, the essentially tragic vision of the poet is revealed. So revealed, even the gay poems now seem sad, almost despairing, and their gaiety, once rejected as forced and false, now also seems frantic. Attention now focuses less on the fanciful and more on the facts of life. The poet's call for fun and festivity, as in "Thieves Kitchen," is now heard together with his closing admonition to the "Cyprian Maids" and the "brave lads of gold" that "your lives are short," so "gulp deep/Those goblets of thick ale—yea, feast and sport," for:

> . . . soon, soon your flesh must crawl
> And Tyburn flap with birds, long-necked and swart! (25)

Several of these early poems end with this fact of death, of men's insignificance and ceasing to be—of the blackness of space swallowing the stars, of the darkness closing in on the sun and on man. Ending the poems this way, Slessor sometimes seems to fool us, for, in the beginning he entices and narcotizes us with vivid images of beauty, vitality, and life; then, when he "has" us, he reveals the end, and all is changed.

Yet Slessor's art is such that we feel that the poet himself has been taken in by the appearance of things, only to be confronted by the realities. Thus, in "Stars," Slessor himself, both as the "passionate poet" within the poem and the poet writing about him, seems dazzled by "the warm candles of beauty, hung in blessing on high." And, at the end, he too seems engulfed by the horror of the black space in-between, the "tunnels of nothingness." Thus, also, in "The Ghost," the poet participates in wild revelry, only to be stopped by the sudden revelation that his host is death, a ghost looking in from the outside at a party he had summoned and was exhilarating in, wishing "to be there alive,/Breathing again!" Unsettling to us but seemingly equally so to the poet, is the sudden transition to a closing couplet, spare, sterile, and dry, from six quatrains filled with the lushness of life: of "old Spanish wine" in "flagons with silver lids," of "music and candleshine," of "fat kitchen-boys" and "maidens like winds of lace," of "platters [that] fume . . . and bottles [that] drip,/ Staining with smoke and spume/Lips, tables, tapestries . . . ." Without warning, the poem ends, assigning in the couplet all the expressions of life to an unexpected host: "So the ghost cried, and pressed to the dark pane,/Like a white leaf, his face . . . in vain . . . in vain . . ." (27).

Unsettling though it is, these vivid and sudden contrasts serve Slessor. The careful building up of color, sounds, smells, the very drippings of life and then their draining into death act to accentuate a voice that speaks out of the dark side of the soul. "In vain . . . in vain" cried the ghost, all is for naught and all will disappear into nothingness. This is true not only for revelers and roistering, as in "The Ghost," but also for decent men and their dreams and deliberations, as in "Taoist." The poet knows that:

> Repenting always of forgotten wrongs
> Will never bring thy heart to rest, for thought
> Repairs no whit of evil; rather cast
> Thy meditations in that utter void
> To which all human deeds resolve at last . . . (6)

Slessor develops to dissipate, builds to break, as life, in its apparent absurdity, seems to do. He moves all to change and disintegration. He does this even in a very short poem like "A Sunset," a poem that follows "Thief of the Moon" in the *Earth-Visitors* volume. Here, the poet first makes us conscious of the life and light aspects of the "sun": "The old Quarry, Sun, with bleeding scales,/Flaps up the gullies, wets their crystal pebbles,/ Floating with waters of gold. . . ." But then almost immediately, for the poem has only eleven lines, he gives us the death and dark aspects of the "set":

> . . . now everything is changed—
> Trees ringed with death, the creek with its bells clanking
> Dried like white bone. Even our voices are estranged.
> Darkness chokes the river; so nearly what I am thinking
> It echoes, the whole thing might have been arranged! (31)

Of course, men still take their turns at life, despite the darkness that chokes the river and echoes their end. They have a part to play, and in the poem, "Next Turn," they play it, in a "Theatre of Varieties." Inevitably, though, they must leave the stage, feeling the "frozen fingers" of the "Footmen" on their sleeves and hearing a most respectful, "Now, Sir, please!" And waiting: "Out in the night, the Carriage stands,/Plumed with black trees . . ." (29). Again, the ultimate darkness, waiting to close in, and life sensed as a journey into the darkness toward oblivion. Yet Slessor's touch is still fanciful in "Next Turn." There is a hectic quality already in evidence as "the flour-faced Antic runs from sight," and something sinister about the grin of the post-boys who wait with the dark carriages. But the "buried pipes" of Pan that "ring out". and the presence of "Colombine with scarlet pout" lightens the poem.

No such lightness nor reference to inhabitants of never-never land remain in "The Night-Ride," perhaps the best of the *Earth-Visitors* poems and among the first of Slessor's "Australian" poems. In "The Night-Ride," the poet takes his imagery directly out of the Australian night at a country station, a train pausing at the platform. The poem, of the here and now (Australia, 1919-26), assigns no special role to the train's anonymous passengers: they simply live and, in the living of "The Night-Ride," they move deeper into the darkness toward oblivion. And with them moves the poet, the "I," seeing nothing but blackness; he moves with them. The detached director of the "Theatre of Varieties" of "Next Turn" has lost his detachment; in "The Night-Ride," Slessor's very emotions seem to mingle with the movement of the train on which man rides rapidly into nothingness:

> Gas flaring on the yellow platform; voices running up and down;
> Milk-tins in cold dented silver; half-awake I stare,
> Pull up the blind, blink out—all sounds are drugged;
> The slow blowing of passengers asleep;
> Engines yawning; water in heavy drips;
> Black, sinister travellers, lumbering up the station,
> One moment in the window, hooked over bags;
> Hurrying, unknown faces—boxes with strange labels—
> All groping clumsily to mysterous ends,
> Out of the gaslight, dragged by private Fates.
> Their echoes die. The dark train shakes and plunges;
> Bells cry out; the night-ride starts again.
> Soon I shall look out into nothing but blackness,
> Pale, windy fields. The old roar and knock of the rails
> Melts in dull fury. Pull down the blind. Sleep. Sleep.
> Nothing but grey, rushing rivers of bush outside.
> Gaslight and milk-cans. Of Rapptown[51] I recall nothing else. (31)

If "The Night-Ride" is among the best of Slessor's early poems, it is because the poet, to an extent more completely than before, has committed all his sensibilities to responding to a world of his own experience. That which has moved him, the poem's very impulse and starting point, has come from what he knows and sees and feels. The poem is good and meaningful also because there is present in it, as there is in a few of the other *Earth-Visitors* poems discussed, a sense of concern as well as craft, a vision of man and his life. However, here, the vision is presented more effectively than before, evolving naturally, rather than through the use of sudden contrasts. In "The Night-Ride" the vision or universal concern emerges from the language representing the poet's response to the local scene: the vision is not imposed upon the poem; it grows out of it. That is, the poem seems successful not because Slessor has "bluntly set out to find a viable analogy for his vision of life," as the young Australian poet, Chris Wallace-Crabbe has analyzed, but rather "because it starts from a clear definition of local and specific perceptions."

[Slessor's] magnificent verbal gifts are no longer wasted on the erection of pleasure domes in Neverneverland, but are devoted to recording the colours, shapes, surfaces of familiar things. One is first of all aware of a particular country station meticulously yet selectively sketched in: yellow lights, silver milk-cans, smoke, luggage, anonymous travellers.[52]

But then, gradually, after this organization of detail about which there is "an emotional weighting . . . somehow suggestive, even mildly sinister," the note of the poem broadens to embrace the vision.

Impressive as "The Night-Ride" are some of the twelve sequences in "Music," the longest poem in *Earth-Visitors* with the exception of "The Man of Sentiment." "Music" is, in fact, in a variety of ways, more significant in pointing to the Slessor of the immediate years to follow who was to introduce modernism into Australian poetry. Originally the second poem in *Earth-Visitors* after "Winter-Dawn," "Music" was chosen by Slessor for his collection, *One Hundred Poems* (1944), to be the final poem of his first period, from 1919 to 1926. This was a felicitous choice, as was the poet's selection of "Earth-Visitors" to be the introductory "set-piece" poem for the period. In the wide range of styles, forms, and moods represented in the twelve sequences, there is a summing-up of both the excesses of the young poet and the growing restraint and control over craft of the maturing one. And in this variety of Slessor's poetic expression is seen the early experimenter, the young poet who, conscious of the traditional forms, began seeking new ones, began a "considered breaking of the rules"[53] which were to demonstrate new possibilities for the Australian poet.

Slessor, with his typical openness to discussing his poetry, has described in "Writing Poetry: The Why and the How" many of his intentions in "Music." They relate to "form," one of the "practical considerations" which have "guided" him for many years. And by form, Slessor means:

. . . that shape of a work, whether in music, words or design, which seems most nearly to reflect the shape of emotion which produced it. Thus, for example, a sonnet, one of the severest formal forms of poetry, is particularly suited in its mechanism for the kind of feeling which possessed Michael Drayton when he wrote the poem beginning "Since there's no help, come, let us kiss and part." On the other hand, there is another kind of emotion which can be matched only by the paradox of disciplined formlessness.[54]

In the twelve-poem sequence "Music," Slessor seeks a variety of forms to "reflect the shape" of his emotions. For one sequence, the fourth, he says: "I tried to find a form to express the monotony and the loneliness of a stream of water running through flat, empty, manless, enormous plains—and I tried to do this by using a flat, monotonous rhythm with a down-fall at the end of each line's last double-syllabled words."[55] Thus:

> In the pans of straw-coned country
>   This river is the solitary traveller;
> Nothing else moves, the sky lies empty,
>   Birds there are none, and cattle not many.
> Now it is sunlight, what is the difference?
>   Nothing. The sun is as white as moonlight.
> Wind has buffeted flat the grasses,
>   Long, long ago; but now there is nothing,
> Wind gone and men gone, only the water
>   Stumbling over the stones in silence . . . (35)

Reading the poem and recalling how nature frequently echoes the poet's feelings, as in "A Sunset" (31), we sense the reflection of Slessor's emotion in his stated concern to find a form that would express the "monotony and loneliness" of a stream running through an empty country. And one sees how the poet's somber emotion is served by a spare, simple, unrhymed form of unstated, restrained language, devoid of life and color. The result is similar to that achieved in "The Night-Ride": a poetic response evoked by *local* conditions which, in the fullness of the poet's emotionality and technical skill, takes on a larger, *universal* meaning. Thus, the physical "Wasteland" that makes up much of Australia, becomes the spiritual "Wasteland" of the soul and of the life of modern man.

If form can be used to express monotony and sterility, to depict a "Wasteland," form also can be used, Slessor says, to "reflect excitement, movement and colour," as in sequence V of Music," a scene from Stravinsky's "Fair." "Form here," the poet says, "depends on the confections of rhyme with a strong, quick, music-hall beat, and is, in fact, quite traditional in its formality":[56]

> In and out the countryfolk, the carriages and carnival,
>   Pastry-cooks in all directions push to barter their confections,
> Trays of little gilded cakes, caramels in painted flakes,
>   Marzipan of various makes and macaroons of all complexions,
> Riding on a tide of country faces.
>
> Up and down the smoke and crying,
>   Girls with diamond[57] eyes are flying,
> Country boys in costly braces
>   Run with red, pneumatic faces;
> Trumpets gleam, whistles scream,
>   Organs cough their coloured steam out,
> Dogs are worming, sniffing, squirming;
>   Air-balloons and paper moons,
> Roundabouts with curdled tunes,
>   Drowned bassoons and waggon-jacks . . . (36)

Form, of course, is only one of the practical considerations which guided Slessor. "Experiment" was another. "With these attempts to unify a poem's emotion with its form," he says, "I also had no hesitation in using Experiment." By Experiment, he means:

a considered breaking of rules where the fracture can suggest even a shadow of the effect desired. The traditional grammar of rhyme, metre and formality must be learnt by any poet as earnestly as the pianist learns his five-finger exercises. But he must not be shackled by academic rules once he has learnt their discipline. The colour and texture of vowel-sounds, the infinite rhythm of consonants, the emotional effects obtained by avoiding a rhyme, approaching a rhyme or by subtly altering it—all these are experiments in anarchy of which poets today know very little except by intuitive feeling.[58]

Slessor goes on to apply these "experiments in anarchy" to the Chopin sequence in "Music," but before he does so he demonstrates their later application to both a poem of his middle period and one of his last. The inclusion of three poems from three periods provides us with an opportunity to judge the poet's growth in craft.

In "Crow Country" (from *Cuckooz Contrey,* 1932) Slessor's *form* "is that of a traditional sonnet shortened by one foot," but he has also tried, he says, "an experiment in the feeling of dreariness and solitude by using only two vowels in the rhyme— the two monotonous sounds of "o" and "i":[59]

> Gutted of station, noise alone,
> The crow's voice trembles down the sky
> As if this nitrous flange of stone
> Wept suddenly with such a cry;
> As if the rock found lips to sigh,
> The riven earth a mouth to moan;
> But we that hear them, stumbling by,
> Confuse their torments with our own.
>
> Over the huge abraded rind,
> Crow-countries graped with dung, we go,
> Past gullies that no longer flow
> And wells that nobody can find,
> Lashed by the screaming of the crow,
> Stabbed by the needles of the mind. (69)

Then, again, in the later "Cock-Crow" (from *Five Bells,* 1939) the more skillful Slessor attempts "to express the sense of remoteness and great distance which comes sometimes in a dream." He does this "by using half-rhymes with an interlocking system of repeated vowel sounds and consonant sounds."[60] Thus:

> The cock's far cry
> From lonely yards
> Burdens the night
> With boastful birds
> That mop their wings
> To make response—
> A mess of songs
> And broken sense.
>
> So, when I slept,
> I heard your call
> (If lips long dead
> Could answer still)
> And snapped-off thoughts

Broke into clamour,
Like the night's throats
Heard by a dreamer. (92)

"In the same way," the poet says, "the remote, unfinished, frustrated feeling of some of Chopin's music is expressed [in a poem from the early "Music" series] by means of half-rhymes which echo with their vowels but not their consonants. You will notice," Slessor says, "how 'channels' is matched by 'planets,' 'festival' by 'emptiness' and so on:[61]

Nothing grows on the stone trees
    But lanterns, frosty gourds of colour,
Melting their bloody drops in water
    Over the dark seas.

These peaks of stucco, smoking light,
    These Venice-roads, the pools and channels,
Tunnel the night with a thousand planets,
    Daubing their glaze of white . . .

Faintly the dripping, crystal strings
    Unlock their Spanish airs, their festival
Which far away resolves to emptiness,
    Echoes of bitter things.

Far away music, cold and small,
    Which, like a child's delight remembered,
Falls to mocked effigy for ever,
    Melancholy to recall. (39-40)

"Music" serves as a bridge from the early to the later poems, but Slessor, in his analysis, makes no distinction between it and the other poems of *Earth-Visitors* and the verse included in *Cuckooz Contrey* (1932) and *Five Bells* (1939). In this discussion of the late forties about the "why and how" of his poetry, the poet no longer attaches periods of composition to his poems (1919-26, 1927-32, 1932-39) as he did when he first brought his three collections together in *One Hundred Poems* (1944). Already, just a few years afterward, Slessor blurs the boundaries between the specific periods of his poetic life and looks at

his work as a unified whole. This is to be his practice henceforth, and in the first of the almost continual flow of reprints
beginning in the fifties (under the title, *Poems*), the poet says
simply: "[The poems] range in date from 1919 to 1947," the
later date covering a few short poems that were initially published in *Southerly* magazine.

There is value in looking back at the *Earth-Visitors* volume
from the later and larger body of the poet's verse. We already
have seen how our understanding of the poems published in the
Vision magazine and anthology is enhanced when they are read
along with those of *Earth-Visitors*. We hear more clearly, for
example, the frantic note in "Thieves Kitchen"; we sense almost
visually the looming abyss behind the lightness of "Adventure
Bay." With Slessor's later poetry in hand, we are able to see that
even at his "first voluptuous feast in the halls of *Vision*":

. . . the poet was deeply conscious of the skull grinning mouthlessly
on the banqueting table, and [that] this grim *memento more* is the
constant element in all his work, giving it an undercurrent of bitter
continuity.[62]

Certainly Slessor's vision of the plight of modern man in
Earth-Visitors is more vivid and pervasive in the light of
Cuckooz Contrey (1932) and *Five Bells* (1939). For the Slessor
of the "Stars" and "The Night-Ride" can be located in the later
Slessor of "Five Bells" who cries out against his friend's and
man's death (and his own) and wishes he could find an answer
or a meaning to man's living and dying: ". . . why you were here/
Who now are gone, what purpose gave you breath." (106). This
vision of the movement of man toward nothingness relates to the
poet's preoccupation in later poems with the passing of time
and his search for permanence in the flux of the present. Here,
too, in *Earth-Visitors*, can be detected the beginnings of this
concern. In "Music" (sequence VIII), "Time is put to rout" and
the gods thwarted by lovers reborn, "clasped each to each."
In "Clocks" "Time is a tide that runneth like to blood/Piping
in human hearts." And at "Nuremberg" in a quiet, high sun
steeped room "only in blown music from the town's/Quaint horo-
loge could Time intrude . . . you'd say/Clocks had been bolted
out, the flux of years/Defied."[63]

Earth-Visitors, viewed together with the later volumes, also points up Slessor's early interest in the life of the city; an interest unique for the time not only in poetry but for Australian literature in general. Perhaps the poet's impulse comes less directly from the city, in "Nuremberg" or "Heine in Paris," and more, as he has indicated, "second-hand" from his readings. Possibly also, in these poems there is something of that which Max Harris calls "a turning back to his paternal heritage of German sensibility"; Harris sees a similar familial relationship to "Music" in which Slessor "turned to associate himself with his Kapell-meister ancestors."[64]

But there seems little question that "Winter Dawn," "City Nightfall," and "Melbourne" (this last poem fortunately omitted from the later collections) grew out of a direct and sustained response to the city. The older Slessor was to have an enduring affair in his poetry with the life of Sydney, more specifically with the built-up area overlooking Sydney Harbor called Kings Cross, an area roughly equivalent to that of Washington Square's "Greenwich Village" in New York. Intimately he was to know the streets below, their very smells and sights: the "puffs of paraffin that crimp the nose," the neons of "pulsing arrows and the running fire."[65]

Slessor was to draw sustenance also from the land beyond the neon, from the spirit of the "Country Towns" (from *Cuckooz Contrey*) with their "willows and squares/And farmers bouncing on barrel mares/To public-houses of yellow wood/With '1860' over their doors." (71) And he was to respond in *Five Bells* to the physicality of the land, of the "South Country" with its "whey-faced anonymity/Of river-gums and scribbly-gums and bush," and of the "North Country" "filled with gesturing wood,/With trees that fence, like archers' volleys,/The flanks of hidden valleys/Where nothing's left to hide" (93-94). This, too, is promised, to some extent, in *Earth-Visitors,* in the poems, "The Night-Ride" and in "Music" (sequence IV) with its "pans of straw-coned country" where the "river is the solitary traveller."

Yet, if Slessor's poetry after *Earth-Visitors* shows increasing intimacy with the city of Sydney and a deepening appreciation of the country towns and bush outside, it is more specifiically Sydney Harbor that engages the maturing poet most enduringly in subsequent volumes. "I haven't gone to sea," Slessor said in a radio interview in 1962, "but I've lived next to water all my life [and] I shall always have Sydney Harbour fixed in my skull."[66] This is hardly true of the poems in *Earth-Visitors:* the Harbor per se is not at all present except in "Winter Dawn" in which the poet says "At five I wake, rise, rub on the smoking pane/A port to see—water breathing in the air." But then, by and large, in *Earth-Visitors* the *pane* through which Slessor frequently peers is still a *Vision* pane and it is difficult for him to see the real water of the Harbor through the bubbling wine of the gods.

The open sea beyond the Heads, as well as Sydney Harbor itself, also becomes increasingly meaningful in the later poems. From the refuge of the harbor, the poet, in the last volume, will listen to a ship's bells and relive the life of a friend long dead. In the process he will relive his own life and that of man, seeking life's meaning and purpose. But first, in *Cuckooz Contrey,* the poet must go to the open sea, outside the Great Barrier Reef to the north. There he will join with the explorer Cook and his men in their search for Australia. In this search Slessor will be moved to explore more fully the realities of the world and to let go of some of the artificial concerns that lingered from the Lindsayite experience.

CHAPTER 3

The Middle Period: 1927-1932
The Poems in Cuckooz Contrey

The first wave of modernism in verse—the verse represented by T. S. Eliot—did not reach these shores [Australia] in any unmistakable form until the publication of Slessor's *Cuckooz Contrey,* as late as 1932.

So wrote the late H. M. Green, Australia's most important literary historian, in his introduction to *Modern Australian Poetry.*[1] We would not quarrel with this judgment which, almost two decades after it was made, still seems essentially sound and unchallengeable. Yet, rereading Slessor and Eliot, we would prefer to underemphasize the phrase, "the verse represented by T. S. Eliot" and say simply, "The first wave of modernism." What seem to be Eliotian echoes may be present, in part, in *Cuckooz Contrey*[2] and perhaps in one or two poems in *Earth-Visitors,* but the influence should not be too quickly assigned. Nor should Slessor's own "waste land," which first emerged from his description of Australia's "straw-coned country" where nothing moves and "the sky lies empty," be viewed simply as "an application of T. S. Eliot's poetic temper to a waste land which exists to the west of Dubbo [place in New South Wales]."[3] Slessor's verse (number IV in the "Music" series), unrhymed and casually reminiscent of Eliot's in its use of simple, understated colloquial language, was written between 1919 and 1926, and though Eliot's "Waste Land" was available in Australia in the early twenties, Slessor did not read it until 1928. "I first read some of Eliot's early poems," Slessor has recently recalled, "in (I think) Amy Lowell's magazine of poetry published in the '20's and read his 'Waste Land' in 1928." And:

Though I admired many of Eliot's technical feats, I was never consciously influenced by him and was, indeed, annoyed by the incoherence and preciosity of parts of the "Waste Land." Yet I appre-

ciated his break from the traditional poetry of the '20's, just as I
appreciated the break made by Harold Monroe, the Sitwells, Robert
Graves, Ezra Pound, William Carlos Williams, Conrad Aiken and
others. But the poets I most admired and tried to emulate at this
period were Robert Frost and Edward Thomas. And I still do.[4]

I Slessor and the "Moderns"

Slessor read deeply in the work of the moderns, British and
American, but his best poetry, when it burgeons forth in *Cuckooz
Contrey,* is distinctly his own. Of course he was touched by his
contemporaries, including Eliot, and various poems in the
volumes, especially as they express experimentation in rhyme,
reflect his readings. But Slessor, for the most part, seemed aware
of and controlled these influences. He "tried to emulate Robert
Frost";[5] he was enthusiastic about "the remarkable poems of
Wilfred Owen" whose "modern experiments in rhyming" were
"the most promising of this century."[6] As earlier in the *Vision*
and *Earth-Visitors* periods, Slessor seemed able to select his
influences and submit them to a creative process from which
emerged poems uniquely his, recognizably Slessorian.

The "first wave of modernism" in verse which H. M. Green
has Slessor bringing to Australia via *Cuckooz Contrey,* was
sighted earlier in *Earth-Visitors.* In the note of disillusionment
which suddenly breaks through in the third stanza of the first
poem, "Winter Dawn," Slessor is already part of the modern
tradition in which literature becomes more and more a record
of "our lonely isolation in the midst of a universe which knows
nothing of us."[7] Similarly, in his appreciation of Eliot's (and
others') "break from the traditional poetry of the '20's,"[8] and in
his own experimentation in the last poems of the volume,
"Music," Slessor is an active participant in the new age "of the
break-up of old forms and the creation of new ones."[9]

Slessor's early modernism is particularly vivid when contrasted
to the anti-modernism of his companions in the *Vision* movement.
In fact, in almost the precise terms that he first exercised his
modernity, they opposed it. For *Vision* stood for:

a repudiation of the negative attitudes of modernist poetry, then
typified by T. S. Eliot, and deplored the "slovenly cleverness" of the
new verse. It asserted instead a lusty vitality devoted to beauty
through traditionally evolved forms.[10]

In this difference from his fellows, we see again Slessor's selective and tentative participation in the Lindsayian world.

Slessor was not only temperamentally a "modern" and an early practitioner of modernism in verse, he was also an ardent spokesman for it. In an address to the Australian English Association some months before the publication of *Cuckooz Contrey*, he stated very clearly his position on the new poetry. Discussing "Experiments in Modern English Poetry," he said:

In what I propose to quote from the work of modern writers, no doubt there is much that is unmusical and graceless. For the fruit of some of these experiments, I feel a violent distaste. None the less, I welcome them more readily than the harvests of stagnation; I would prefer my feelings to be outraged by Mr. E. E. Cummings, rather than have my intellect candied into stupor by Mr. Edward Shanks. I regard the silliest, the vulgarest, the crudest of the moderns as of more value than the literary Shintoists who cumber up anthologies with their trance-like worshipping of ancestors.[11]

"Worshipping" or automatic aping of the older English poets, a practice of many of the literary Australian poets of the time, was an anathema to Slessor. What he sought was sincerity— the poet's effort to express his emotions in his *own* terms. It was not simply a search for newness, for new forms and images; rather, it was more a process of arriving at them through one's own struggle. "Certain images," for example, Slessor said:

. . . have been sanctified by the dynasty of English poets; if a modern writer employs one of these figures because he has discovered an eternal truth for himself—if, for instance, he says the moon is "like a sickle" because he has seen both a sickle and a moon, and the similarity has burst upon him—his line will gain in sincerity something of what it loses in originality: if, on the other hand, he compares the moon to a sickle merely because such an exercise has been pardoned by established precedent, he is guilty of the worst kind of intellectual dishonesty, and will not be able to disguise it in his verse. The traditions of the present are the experiments of the past; to rest on them is to deny a future.[12]

Slessor, as a modern, was reaching out for his own vision and seeking means to express it. Yet he would not discard the past out of hand; he had respect for it and would use it. "I do not wish it to be thought that the traditional forms, the inherited orthodoxies, are to be scorned by modern writers," he said:

Movement in poetry is to be áchieved by a gradual building process, a subtle variation of modes and patterns already canonized. There can be no sudden explosion of revolt, such as is attempted by the incendiaries under the domination of Cummings and Gertrude Stein. Even T. S. Eliot obtains his most powerful poetry by a simple inflection or variation of the standardized pentameter.[13]

In this pioneering address on modern poetry to "a gathering of about forty members"[14] of the Australian English Association at a special meeting presided over by H. M. Green, then Librarian at Sydney University, Slessor quoted directly and explained in detail work from Eliot, Marianne Moore, Harold Monroe, E. E. Cummings, and Wilfred Owen. In doing so, he revealed not only his close reading of these poets and others, but also his point of view about the purpose of various technical aspects of poety. For example, with reference to rhymes:

Poetry's [traditional] concern with rhythm is its employment as a sort of hypnotic agent which will urge the mind to vibrate at a deeper level of consciousness than that of the superficial world.

However:

The rhythms and cadences which have been attempted in modern poetry are very distant from the orthodox measures of the past. Their analysis, in some cases, is almost impossible; yet their success in these cases is generally plain to even a prejudiced reader.[15]

Slessor, to illustrate, then quoted from what he called "the extraordinary and unforgettable opening" of Eliot's "Waste Land" which, despite his annoyance with the "incoherence and preciosity of some of its parts," was "filled with the most splendid and haunting rhythms of anything written in our century."[16]

II   Comments on Technique

That Slessor was not only very knowledgeable about the modern poets, but that he was also a student of the history of modernism itself, a remarkably informed one for an Australian poet of the time, was also indicated in the discussion. Slessor saw, as an instance, that modern free-verse rhythms had been developing for many years, and that it was possible:

to trace a dynastic growth, from Whitman to Mallarmé, to the French Imagistes, to Ezra Pound of 1912, to the American Imagists, to the English Richard Aldington, to the writer who calls herself H. D., to Amy Lowell, to Mr. Cummings himself.[17]

But, simultaneously, Slessor was aware that many other experiments in rhythm were being made, within "restricted boundaries," by other poets who have never committed themselves to free verse. An example is to be found in A. E. Housman, whose book of lyrics, *A Shropshire Lad*, "so enormously influenced the stream of modern English poetry. Housman conceived the idea of adding a fifth line to the conventional quatrain, giving it a half-sad and reflective echo that was supremely successful. James Flecker, linked in the popular mind with Rupert Brooke, but an infinitely greater poet, made several experiments with Eastern verse-forms, and achieved his loveliest result with 'Yasmin.' In addition, he thoroughly explored the scope of the English hexameter. His translations in this form offer an interesting contrast with Tennyson's experiment in quantity."[18]

Tennyson, incidentally, mentioned here in passing, was to be acknowledged later by Slessor as his "master,"—"a teacher and master of metrical genius . . . to whom any poet can go for lessons in technique."[19] No such indebtedness was yet expressed in Slessor's early address before the Australian English Association, but of the poets discussed, he seemed most impressed with Wilfred Owen, the soldier-poet who was killed during the closing days of World War I; to the thirty-year-old Slessor, Owen's modern experiments in rhyming were "the most promising of the century." Slessor used variations of these experiments in various poems in *Cuckooz Contrey*, and it is revealing to place the poems against his analysis of Owen's work. Owen, Slessor said:

relied for an effect of rhyme on carefully-arranged schemes of assonance and dissonance, together with a sort of inverted assonance which depended on the partial matching of consonants and not vowels. His experiments succeeded triumphantly in his greatest poem, 'Strange-Meeting':

Now men will go content with what we spoiled,
Or, discontent, boil bloody, and be spilled.
They will be swift with swiftness of the tigress,
None will break ranks, though nations trek from progress.
Courage was mine, and I had mystery,
Wisdom was mine, and I had mastery;
To miss the march of this retreating world
Into vain citadels that are not walled.

"The effect of these rhymed consonants," Slessor observed, "as in 'spoiled' and 'spilled,' 'tigress' and 'progress,' produces a grave and sombre music that is perfectly fitted to the poem." In addition:

Owen added to this feeling of majestic despair by starting each couplet with the longer-sounding vowels, and using shorter-sounding vowels in the second line, thus giving an impression of sadness and lassitude.[20]

Slessor then illustrated how he attempted to relate a variation of Owen's experimentation to his own "The Country Ride" from *Cuckooz Contrey.* "By way of variation," he said,

I have tried, not the matching of consonants only or vowels only, but the repetition of a whole syllable, both vowels and consonants, so that it is not a rhyme but really the same word, or portion of the same word, reiterated.[21] [For example]:

Earth which has known so many passages
Of April air, so many marriages
Of strange and lovely atoms breeding light,
Never may find again that lost delight.

In the sharp sky, the frosty deepnesses,
There are still birds to barb the silences,
There are still fields to meet the morning on,
But those who made them beautiful have gone . . . (75)

Though many are mentioned in the AEA address, Owen was the only modern whom Slessor related directly to his own work. In one instance, however, he did couple a poem by Marianne Moore with one from *Cuckooz Contrey,* "Fixed Ideas," as an illustration of the kind of form which modern poetry was taking.

"Fixed Ideas" (later changed to "Fixed Opinions") was to be offered on subsequent occasions[22] by the poet as a prime example of the artist disciplining his form to serve his purpose. On these occasions, he was to answer questions about the meaning of the poem—about which there was much confusion—with detailed explanations. This first time, though, after quoting the poem, he simply offered:

the idea is fundamentally a contrast between the solidity and stiffness of rigid opinion, and the fluidity of the real stream of thought which besieges the human brain. The contrast is emphasized by the abrupt change from the first part, with its long, heavy lines, to the rapidly-running short lines of the second part.[23]

To illustrate:

> Ranks of electroplated cubes, dwindling to glitters,
> Like the other pasture, the trigonometry of marble,
> Death's candy-bed. Stone caked on stone,
> Dry pyramids and racks of iron balls.

is contrasted with

> Frail tinkling rush
> Water-hair streaming
> Prickles and glitters
> Cloudy with bristles
> River of thought
> Swimming the pebbles—
> Undo, loosen your bubbles! (74)

Elsewhere, in a humorous aside, Slessor will tell us that the last line of the poem, "Undo, loosen your bubbles!" was always said to him by an old friend when he met him at the counter in the pub. He appealed to Slessor to do this and to buy him a glass of beer.[24]

The researcher, looking for a fuller understanding of the poet and his poems, not just the technician and his techniques, would gladly "shout" (an Australianism for "treat") both Slessor and friend to beers if, in the "loosening up" process, Slessor would talk about the "Whys' of his writing poetry; his emphasis seems always on the "Hows." To Slessor, this is perfectly logical. "To discuss the 'Why' poets write poetry," he says, in "Writing Poetry: The Why and the How," "would be an excursion beyond psychology into the springs of life of which I am not capable." Rather, he is content "to talk as lucidly as I can about the tiny area of the 'How' of which I know anything."[25]

Slessor does more than this. Though a private man, he is not only generous in discussing the craft of his work, but also, when pertinent, background information from his personal and professional life. Relating to the verse of the middle period, the verse of *Cuckooz Contrey*, we know, for example (for Slessor has told us), that the "Captain," in "Captain Dobbin," his first major poem, is based "in some ways" on "an old, retired sea captain, who had an astonishing knowledge of nautical things." We know also that this same sea-captain, Captain Francis Bayldon, who "was my wife's uncle," helped to inspire him to write "Five Visions of Captain Cook," one of Slessor's greatest poems and among the most influential ones in Australian literature. For Slessor has told us that on weekly visits to Captain Bayldon, he was allowed to browse through the captain's magnificent nautical library, and that over a glass of sherry he was encouraged to ask the captain questions.[26]

Nor, when it might be helpful to the reader, will Slessor hesitate to recall quite personal incidents from his early childhood. There are the "long journeys," for example, "by coach from one bush village to another" with his father, an English-born mining engineer,[27] which may explain, in part, the nostalgia that dilutes the satire in his lovely "Country Towns" where:

> At the School of Arts, a broadsheet lies
> Sprayed with the sarcasm of flies:
> "The Great Golightly Family
> Of Entertainers Here To-night"—
> Dated a year and a half ago,
> But left there, less from carelessness
> Than from a wish to seem polite. (71)

To Slessor these memories of childhood and his discussions about Cook with Captain Bayldon are factual and, being such, are acceptable and worthy of sharing with the reader; a trained journalist, he is familiar and comfortable with facts, will seek them and stay with them. Simultaneously, therefore, he will not speculate nor will he enter the confessional. Striving always for his own special lucidity, Slessor will not leap into faith or speculation: he simply will not deal with the "Why."

Yet, in the same article in which he dedicates his full energies to discuss the "How" of his verse, Slessor does allow us a glimpse into his motivations as a poet. Fearful that his "dissection of how [his poetry] works" will "sound like a talk from a laboratory," Slessor prefaces his discussion with:

I think poetry is written mostly for pleasure, by which I mean the pleasure of pain, horror, anguish and awe as well as the pleasure of beauty, music and the act of living.

And closes with:

But I must write for myself, and speak for myself, and that is why writing poetry is still, I think, a pleasure out of hell.[28]

These "Why" comments add to our appreciation of Slessor's poetry, and we are grateful for them. Ultimately, though, it is to the poems themselves, not Slessor's words about them, that we must look for our larger understanding of the man and the poet and the meaning of his poems. Slessor's poems offer such possibilities of discovery, for, "more than any other writer in Australia, Slessor is a man who is illuminated through his poetry."[29] This is particularly true of poems written during the middle period of *Cuckooz Contrey* and later in *Five Bells*. They reveal not only the "Why" of Slessor's verse and demonstrate the "How," but also suggest reasons, in addition to craft, for Slessor's apparent preoccupation with the "How." Certainly, in doing so, they also highlight Slessor the modernist: the technical experimenter, the skeptical and ironical voice, the intelligent man aware and critical of the tragic nature of life.

III *The Poetry of* Cuckooz Contrey

In the work of no Australian poet before Slessor does the reader ultimately become so emotionally aware of the despair, of the sense of alienation and loss that Lionel Trilling sees as marking "The Modern Element in Modern Literature."[30] Nor are

there Australian poets prior to Slessor who seem to hold so
steadily that "vision of a whole situation" which incorporates
the past into the present that Stephen Spender formulated in
The Struggle of the Modern.[31] Or any for whom Gautier's
celebrated phrase for the Modern movement, "c'est que je
suis un homme pour qui le monde visible existe,"[32] seems so
appropriate. The despair, the use of the past, the seizing on
aspects of the visible world—these are interrelated in Slessor's
poetry, and they, in turn, connect to Slessor's concern with the
nature of time and his preoccupation with the sea. Hinted at
in *Earth-Visitors* (1926), all this begins to emerge in *Cuckooz
Contrey* (1932).

Cuckooz Contrey: given Slessor's seriousness and the tragic
sense of things that comes forth from most of the poems in the
volume, we might at first wonder at this title and the delightfully light-spirited poem from which it is drawn. Called "The
King of Cuckooz," the poem is one in a series of five under a
collective title of "The Atlas." In each, Slessor typically quotes
from an old record or nautical journal and then, using it as a
take-off point, builds a poem. For example, in "The King of
Cuckooz" he prefaces the poem with:

[The Platt of Argier and the Pts. adioning within the view thereof
made by Robert Norton the Muster Mr. of his Mat's Fleet ther Ao Di
1620 & by his owne carfull & dilligent observations then not without
danger.]

And then moves directly into the poem with:

> The King of Cuckooz Contrey
> Hangs peaked above Argier
> With Janzaries and Marabutts
> To bid a sailor fear—
>
> With lantern-eyed astrologers
> Who walk upon the walls
> And ram with stars their basilisks
> Instead of cannon-balls.
>
> And in that floating castle
> (I tell you it is so)

> Five thousand naked Concubines
> With dulcimers do go.
>
> .   .   .   .
>
> And this I spied by moonlight
> Behind a royal bamboo—
> That Monarch in a curricle
> Which ninety virgins drew;
>
> That Monarch drinking nectar
> (Lord God, my tale attest!)
> Milked from a snow-white elephant
> As white as *your* white breast! . . . (47)

Similarly, in "Post Roads," the poet first mentions: [The Traveller's Guide, or A Most Exact Description of the Roads of England; being Mr. Ogilby's Actual Survey and Mensuration by the Wheel, &c.]

And then immediately picks up the:

> POST-ROADS that clapped with tympan heels
> Of tilburies and whiskeys rapidly spanking,
> Where's now the tireless ghost of Ogilby? . . . (49)

The original idea for the title poem, "The King of Cuckooz," and possibly for the "Atlas" series itself, seems to have been inspired, in part, at least, by Slessor's discovery of an old map among a variety of old nautical memorabilia through which he habitually browsed. The map gave him the name of the country (spelled "contrey") and his imagination and feelings, the king— and the rest. "The King of Cuckooz" is full of fun and of a zest for life. In fact, in the final stanzas, the poet reminds his lady listener, that though he's "no King of Cuckooz Land," he has

> . . . as huge an appetite,
> As deep a kiss, my girl,
> And *somewhere,* for the hand that seeks,
> Perhaps a Sultan's pearl! (48)

As we dwell on the essentially tragic quality of Slessor's vision, we should appreciate that this "huge appetite" and the high spirits of the poem are not foreign to the poet; certainly, Slessor has a large capacity for pleasure. Always this has been true; there was never anything of the monk about him. The "retired" poet and elder statesman of Sydney journalism, who today presides[33] over the lush and affluent Sydney Journalist Club and enjoys good food and wine and the conversation of close friends, is not too different from the beginning poet and news-paperman whom Jack Lindsay recalls in *The Roaring Twenties*. Already the young Slessor is seen as having proclivities for the good things of life, of dining well, of dressing well, like a "Byronic dandy," of collecting curiosa, of delighting in music and art. And, though he was more fastidious than his friends and "kept aloof from the more knockabout boozers and main-tained his own journalistic routines,"[34] he was a social being, had a wonderful wit, and was a good pub companion. The high-pitched note of "The Mask," for example, a poem Lindsay remembers as having been inspired by conversation in a wine-bar, "was not too high for the level of ardent discovery and companionship we then inhabited."[35]

True, the uninhibited and unmixed humor of "The King of Cuckooz" is rare in Slessor's poetry, but much less rare in the man himself. Not only his fellow poets of the time, but also his old newspaper mates recall his good sense of fun. They re-member particularly both the topical jingles he wrote for *Smith's Weekly*, which are still "rich with their original laughter" and the impeccable light verse about situations and lovely ladies like "Cucumber Kitty" and "Kimono Cora" which attracted sophisticated readers to *Smith's* "who normally would have found little to their taste in the paper."[36]

In a variety of ways, other poems in *Cuckooz Contrey* also express something of the high humor of "The King." "A Bush-ranger" has a hero named "Jackey Jackey" who "gallops on a horse like a swallow/Where the carbines bark and the black-boys hollo.", who "can shoot off hats, for to have a bit of fun,/ With a bulldog bigger than a buffalo-gun" (72). And the poem "La Dame Du Palais De La Reine" has "Sophie, in shocks of scarlet lace,/ [who] "Receives her usual embrace" [and wonders] "whether a kiss be worth the care/Five minions wasted on her hair." In the "Mermaids" (one of the "Atlas" poems), the mermaids are old-established Ladies who no longer "tumble in the sponges of the moon/For the benefit of tourists in the First Saloon" (51). And in "Mephistopheles Perverted (Or Goethe for the Times)" there is a Flea:

> Who kept such a fine, fat King,
> Not that he held with royalty,
> But more for the appearance of the thing. (79)

Certainly, only fun is intended in "A Bushranger," Slessor's gentle mock of the exaggeration and sentimentality of the old Australian ballad. And not much more in "La Dame," though Sophie, recalling the ladies of Lindsay's world, is not so gay. When her lovers come "With books of music, diamond rings,/ Spaniels and roses, fireworks, swings," "Sophie sighs, but thinks 'on Higher Things.'"

"Mermaids," too, is a pleasant poem about the passing of mermaids who once danced in seas "full of Dolphins' fins,/ . . . and flying Jinns," but now "Dance no more." And where once a mariner "Would cast his tranquil eyes/On singular kinds of Hermaphrodites/Without the least surprise," now scientists "with binocular eyes,/Remark in tone of complacent surprise:/"Those pisciform mammals—pure Spectres, I fear—/Must be Doctor Gerbrandus's *Mermaids*, my dear!" (52).

The spirit is light here, too, but we leave the poem with some feeling of sadness and sense of loss. Once there was a time for imagining and dreaming; now it is no more: now we live with the facts, the literalness of things. We will discover this sadness and sense of loss with increasing frequency and depth in many poems of the middle period. Gradually it will suffuse the poem, as in "Elegy in A Botanic Gardens." There, the poet, revisiting the Gardens, recalls the past when he was young and in love, and sees again the "dead grove/Where we had kissed, to the Tristania tree/Where we had kissed so awkwardly,/Noted by swans with damp, accusing eyes." All that is gone today: "only the leaves remain,/Gaunt paddles ribbed with herringbones,/ Of watermelon-pink. . . ." And the very building in the gardens where once romantically there "was no time for botany" is seen at last, realistically, as

> . . . no Georgian Headlong Hall
> With glass-eye windows winking candles forth,

Stuffed with French horns, globes, air-pumps, telescopes
And Cupid in a wig, playing the flute,
But truly, and without escape
THE NATIONAL HERBARIUM, (55)

Like "A Bushranger," "La Dame Du Palais De La Reine,"
and "Mermaids," "Mephistopheles Perverted" also encourages
laughter. Yet, even more than in "Mermaids," Slessor in this
poem wants more than our amusement; he wants us to feel the
bite of his bile:

Such relics [kings] every Flea must flaunt,
If only as the final trump
That mocks Materialism's taunt,
Proving there's more in life than Suck and Jump. (79)

Is there more to life than "Suck and Jump"? More to life than
the physicality of it, the daily living of it, the ultimate dying
of it? Slessor's flea, smug in his righteousness and sense of values,
is more certain of it than the poet. "Who knows," the poet wonders, looking at "The Nabob":

Coming out of India with ten thousand a year
Exchanged for flesh and temper, a dry Faust
Whose devil barters with digestion, has he paid dear
For dipping his fingers in the Roc's valley?

Who knows? It's certain that he owns a rage,
A face like shark-skin, full of Yellow Jack,
And that unreckoning tyranny of age
That calls for turtles' eggs in Twickenham.

Sometimes, by moonlight, in a barge he'll float
Whilst hirelings blow their skulking flageolets.
Served by a Rajah in a golden coat
With pigeon-pie . . . Madeira . . . and Madeira . . .

Or in his Bon de Paris with silver frogs
He rolls puff-bellied in an equipage,
Elegant chariot, through a gulf of fogs
To dine on dolphin-steak with Post-Captains.

> Who knows? There are worse things than steak, perhaps,
> Worse things than oyster-sauces and tureens
> And worlds of provender like painted maps
> Pricked out with ports of claret and pitchcocked eels . . . (76)

Always with wit, but with a sense of weariness and disenchantment that dilutes it, Slessor frequently questions the value of
the higher aspirations. In fact, he seems bored with them and
with himself. "After all, you are my rather tedious hero," he
says in the ironical "To Myself":

> Have you not played Hamlet's father in the wings
> Long enough, listening to poets groan,
> Seeking a false catharsis
> In flesh not yours, through doors ajar
> In the houses of dead kings,
> In the gods' tombs, in the coffins of cracked stone?
>
> Have you not poured yourself, thin fluid mind,
> Down the dried-up canals, the powdering creeks,
> Whose waters none remember
> Either to praise them or condemn,
> Whose fabulous cataracts none can find
> Save one who has forgotten what he seeks?

At least:

> Your uncle, the Great Harry, left after him
> The memory of a cravat, a taste in cheese,
> And a way of saying "I am honoured."
> Such things, when men and beasts have gone,
> Smell sweetly to the seraphim.
> Believe me, fool, there are worse gifts than these. (54)

Burdened with mentality and concerned with the reason for
meanings in life, Slessor sometimes wishes he were someone
else. "Suddenly to become John Benbow," he muses in "Metempsychosis":

> . . . walking down William Street
> With a tin trunk and a five-pound note, looking for a place to eat,
> And a peajacket the colour of a shark's behind
> That a Jew might buy in the morning. . . .

To fry potatoes (God save us!) if you feel inclined,
Or to kiss the landlady's daughter, and no one mind,
In a peel-papered bedroom with a whistling jet
And a picture of the Holy Virgin. . . .

Wake in a shaggy bale of blankets with a fished-up cigarette,
Picking over "Turfbird's Tattle" for a Saturday morning bet,
With a bottle in the wardrobe easy to reach
And a blast of onions from the landing. . . .

.   .   .   .

Banjo-playing, firing off guns, and other momentous things to do,
Such as blowing through peashooters at hawkers to improve
      the view—
Suddenly paid-off and forgotten in Woolloomooloo. . . .

Suddenly to become John Benbow. . . . (78)

John Benbow and William Hickey,[37] the latter to whose memory "The Nabob" was written, are strong men, secure in their
passions and personalities and Slessor admires them. And, if
minded by his consciousness, he is unable to embrace them
completely, the poet will not condemn their excesses. Nor will
he "altogether condemn" Hickey when the latter curses the day
when lusts are left behind: "—God damn your blood!—/Even
his curses I'd not altogether condemn,/Not altogether scorn. . . ."
    Yet, Slessor, with a wit which wastes no words, ironical and
real, would promise the departed Hickey even more:

. . . and if phantoms ate—

Hickey, I'd say, sit down, pull up, set to:
Here's knife and fork, there's wine, and there's a barmaid . . . (77)

Slessor is sympathetic to the need to seize the world by our
senses, to grasp, to taste, to smell, to see and hear that which is
now—for beyond it there seems an eternity of silence and
nothingness. His is a deep capacity for life, and he appreciates
men like Hickey and Benbow who are able to exercise their
life forces freely, for he cannot! Always, as Jack Lindsay recalls
in *The Roaring Twenties*, there was "an inner conflict between
his keen sense of enjoyment and sense of overwhelming loss."[38]

Indeed, we might attribute to Slessor something of the "invincible summer,"[39] the emotional response to immediate life that existed in Albert Camus and saved him from nihilism. Yet, like Camus's Dr. Rieux, Slessor's emotionality is checked by his terrible knowledge: his "clear awareness of man's accidental and transitory presence on earth."[40]

The gay title, then, *Cuckooz Contrey,* seems to express simultaneously Slessor's deep commitment to life and the possibility of its pleasures, and a deeply felt sense of irony that incessantly intrudes from his awareness that all ultimately is for naught. The commitment, or an inclination of it, was present early and encouraged Slessor to live, if somewhat gingerly, with the Lindsayites and the *Vision* cult of gaiety. The irony came later and provided a release for Slessor that helped him to come to terms with his "overwhelming sense of loss." This strengthened his commitment which, in the early poems before the release provided by irony, was frequently forced and hectic. Of course, the fact that Cuckooz Contrey itself, is exotic and remote suggests that the title also may be a kind of *cri de coeur,* a wishing away from the present and the real, for things that no longer are or never were. Certainly also, there is sufficient play of fancy and fantasy in the volume to support the title without the sting.

Yet the sting is necessary; it is precisely intended. For Cuckooz Contrey also incites a Swiftian response, embracing as it does, a place of despair where modern man is without power or hope, "lashed down like Gulliver, with innumerable cables . . . his desires, his limitations, his accidents, his vices, his diseases."[41]

"Hair over hair"—cries Slessor's "Gulliver"—"I pick my cables loose":

But still the ridiculous manacles confine me.
I snap them, swollen with sobbing. What's the use?
One hair I break, ten thousand hairs entwine me.
Love, hunger, drunkenness, neuralgia, debt,
Cold weather, hot weather, sleep and age—

.   .   .   .

I could break my teeth on a chain, I could bite through metal,
But what can you do with hairs?
For God's sake, call the hangman. (73)

Not only Lilliput, but the voyage to Laputa where Gulliver's flesh crept "with a horror I cannot express," is recalled in *Cuckooz Contrey*. In the poem "Glubbdubdrib," a title taken from the voyage, Slessor's darkened vision of the human condition extends beyond the misery of life and its ultimate insignificance in death to a further and unendurable end. There, great men with great minds have been reduced after death to abject slaves of the Glubbdubdribians, the epitome of stupidity and greed.

> "Really, the servant problem . . .
> You mean that Roman youth?
> Catullus. Oh, yes, brisk enough,
> But—you know—so uncouth.
>
> "There's Plato in the passage,
> They tell me he's quite droll.
> He says some devilish clever things;
> A heathen, though, poor soul. . . ."
>
> The governor of Glubbdubdrib
> Resumes his drinking-cup.
> As for the guests and visitors,
> They hadn't even looked up. (66)

Of course, stupidity and greed are also part of a real present which defeats and dehumanizes decent and intelligent men. Slessor has known such good men, is loyal to them, loves them. And, when they die, he startles us (as he often does) into an awareness of the anguish of his loss by the grotesqueness of his imagery, "This little bin of cancelled flesh," he says in "Burying Friends," "Strode the earth once,/Rubbed against men—/But that's all done. . . .:

> Only it seems not a burial
> Of irrelevant sods,
> But a lopped member
> From this my body . . . (68)

The recollection of such lost friends and the memories of times long past are part of Slessor's present. Sometimes they seem almost forgotten by the newspaperman, the special writer for *Smith's Weekly*, preoccupied by the pressures of the day. As frequently, though, they are remembered by the poet of *Cuckooz Contrey*, filling him with a sense of loss. "There are still fields to meet the morning on," he cries in "The Country Ride," "but those who made them beautiful have gone." "Have gone"—the phrase haunts, as the very present reveals that which is precious and missing from the past. In the poem, "Wild Grapes," the poet wanders into:

> The old orchard, full of smoking air,
> Full of sour marsh and broken boughs, is there,
> But kept no more by vanished Mulligans,
> Or Hartigans, long drowned in earth themselves,
> Who gave this bitter fruit their care. (63)

Nothing much grows there now but some wild grapes, Isabella grapes they're called, and "Eating their flesh, half-savage with black fur,/Acid and gypsy-sweet," the poet thinks of "Isabella, the dead girl, who has lingered on/Defiantly when all have gone away,/. . . [Isabella], A girl half-fierce, half-melting as these grapes,/Kissed here . . . but who remembers now?"

Slessor remembers: this is his function as a poet. His is no exalted sense of mission, no role of high priest of the Muse: Slessor does what he has to do, what emotionally he seems compelled to do: he remembers. In the remembering, he keeps alive people and events which time would move along into death and disappearance. And in the recalling of the past, frequently idealized, he helps himself live with a dreary present, which often seems a waste land without hope, a "Crow Country," "graped with dung," where "gullies . . . no longer flow/. . . Lashed by the screaming of the crow,/Stabbed by the needles of the mind" (69). This, too, is part of *Cuckooz Contrey*.

IV *"Captain Dobbin"*

It is of the past and man's remembering and imagining of it from the present that Slessor writes in the two most important poems in *Cuckooz Contrey*, "Five Visions of Captain Cook" and "Captain Dobbin." They are also, together with the later "Five Bells" and "Beach Burial," Slessor's major poems and among the best written in Australian literature. In the two later poems, Slessor will deal directly with the experiences of his own past;

in "Cook" and "Dobbin" of *Cuckooz Contrey* he deals with a
past extending back before his own beginnings to Australia's.
Yet it is a past which seems to belong to Slessor emotionally
no less than to the men for whom he is remembering it. There
is, in fact, little distance between the poet and his persona: indeed, it is the poet's emotions we often feel most strongly.
And these emotions express no mere and usual nostalgiazing of
the past, but involve an embrace of it so completely that the
present is forgotten. This is particularly true in "Captain Dobbin."
The poem, in blank verse, and beautifully illustrative of Slessor's
experimentation with half-rhymes, assonance, and vowel repetition, opens in the here and now. We are introduced to the
Captain:

> CAPTAIN DOBBIN, having retired from the South Seas
> In the dumb tides of 1900, with a handful of shells,
> A few poisoned arrows, a cask of pearls,
> And five thousand pounds in the colonial funds,
> Now sails the street in a brick villa, "Laburnum Villa,"
> In whose blank windows the harbour hangs
> Like a fog against the glass,
> Golden and smoky, or stoned with a white glitter,
> And boats go by, suspended in the pane,
> Blue Funnel, Red Funnel, Messageries Maritimes,
> Lugged down the port like sea-beasts taken alive
> That scrape their bellies on sharp sands,
> Of which particulars Captain Dobbin keeps
> A ledger sticky with ink,
> Entries of time and weather, state of the moon,
> Nature of cargo and captain's name, . . . (42)

Time continues in the present throughout the stanza but the
past has been sensed immediately as existing within it. We have
been told that Captain Dobbin "Now sails the street in a brick
villa." This is a statement of poetic fact, gently satirical though
it be. The old sailor, in mind and heart, still *sails* his ship: his
remembering and love of the past blurs the present. Yet he is
aware of the present and acts within it: he looks out from a
"present" window on the waters of a "present" harbor (as
Slessor did much of his life)[42] and keeps his ledger. The
sea in his mind, however, flowing with the emotions of the

past, is much closer to Dobbin than the actual sea seen outside his window, more real to him than his looking out upon it and keeping track of the ships of the present. This sea, Slessor tells us in the second stanza, is:

> Closer to him than a dead, lovely woman,
> For he keeps bits of it, like old letters,
> Salt tied up in bundles
> Or pressed flat,
> What you might call a lock of the sea's hair,
> So Captain Dobbin keeps his dwarfed memento,
> His urn-burial, a chest of mummied waves,
> Gales fixed in print, and the sweet dangerous countries
> Of shark and casuarina-tree,
> Stolen and put in coloured maps,
> Like a flask of seawater, or a bottled ship,
> A schooner caught in a glass bottle;
> But Captain Dobbin keeps them in books,
> Crags of varnished leather
> Pimply with gilt, by learned mariners
> And masters of hydrostatics, or the childish tales
> Of simple heroes, taken by Turks or dropsy.... (43)

Flooded by memories, as "nightly he sails from shelf to shelf/ Or to the quadrants, dangling with rusty screws,/Or the hanging-gardens of old charts," Dobbin becomes almost totally absorbed in the past, reliving it not nostalgically and sentimentally, but actually. In effect, in the third stanza, the past becomes the present for him. And a vital present it is, compared to the actual one he has been living since his retirement in the long ago of 1900—the exciting and expectant years preceding the birth of the Australian nation—and of Slessor. In this new momentary present Dobbin is once again a young, adventurous sailor who:

> ... felt the barbéd rush
> Of bubbles foaming, spied the albicores,
> The blue-finned admirals, heard the wind-swallowed cries
> Of planters running on the beach
> Who filched their swags of yams and ambergris,
> Birds' nests and sandalwood, from pastures numbed
> By the sun's yellow, too meek for honest theft;
> But he, less delicate robber, climbed the walls,
> Broke into dozing houses

Crammed with black bottles, marish wine
Crusty and salt-corroded, fading prints,
Sparkle-daubed almanacs and playing cards,
With rusty cannon, left by the French outside,
Half-buried in sand . . . (43)

Filling up emotionally with this "living again," but simultaneously becoming conscious again of the actual present, Captain
Dobbin's eye, "That eye of wild and wispy scudding blue,/ . . .
would light up/Like mica scratched by gully-suns,":

And he would be fearful to look upon
And shattering in his conversation;
Nor would he tolerate the harmless chanty,
No "Shenandoah," or the dainty mew
That landsmen offer in a silver dish
To Neptune, sung to pianos in candlelight.
Of these he spoke in scorn,
For there was but one way of singing "Stormalong,"
He said, and that was not really singing,
But howling, rather-shrieked in the wind's jaws
By furious men; not tinkled in drawing-rooms
By lap-dogs in clean shirts. (43-44)

"Lap-dogs in clean shirts"—this is what men have become.
Angry at the thought (and perhaps frightened also as he partially
senses that he too has deteriorated), Dobbin returns to his
mementoes, now: "galleries of photographs, men with rich
beards,/Pea-jackets and brass buttons, with folded arms." And
they scowl approval at Dobbin's point of view "for they were
shipmates, too,/Companions of no cruise by reading glass." They
are not simply dead objects to trigger memory; they have remained almost real and alive, superior to nostalgia. They were
his "fellows of storm and honey from the past." Buoyed by them,
Dobbin again plunges into remembering:

"The Charlotte, Java, '93,"
"Knuckle and Fred at Port au Prince,"
"William in his New Rig,"
Even that notorious scoundrel, Captain Baggs,
Who, as all knew, owed Dobbin Twenty Pounds
Lost at fair cribbage, but he never paid,

Or paid "with the slack of the tops'l sheets"
As Captain Dobbin frequently expressed it. (44)

Dobbin moves into and out of the past. Loving it, he would not leave it, but not leaving it, he would die, and Dobbin does not yet want to die. So the actual present still clutches, not only painful to him when contrasted with the romanticized past, but simultaneously diminishing of that past by its unyielding reality.

In the photographs the faces of his friends are "grilled a trifle now,/Cigar-hued in various spots/By the brown breath of sodium-eating years,/On quarter-decks long burnt to the water's edge,/A resurrection of the dead by chemicals." And all that remains of "the voyages they had made,/Their labours in a country of water," is "marked by inadequate lines/On charts tied up like skins in a rack." Even "his own Odysseys, his lonely travels,/His trading days,"—are they not an "autobiography":

Of angles and triangles and lozenges
Ruled tack by tack across the sheet,
That with a single scratch expressed the stars,
Merak and Alamak and Alpherat,
The wind, the moon, the sun, the clambering sea,
Sails bleached with light, salt in the eyes,
Bamboos and Tahiti oranges,
From some forgotten countless day,
One foundered day from a forgotten month,
A year sucked quietly from the blood, . . . (44)

Is that too not "Dead with the rest, remembered by no more/Than a scratch on a dry chart"? Frustrated by the return to his own past, Dobbin looks further back and recalls those of others, "the wanderings of other keels,/Magellan, Bougainville and Cook," early explorers looking for the unknown continent of Australia. But, they too, ultimately "found no greater a memorial/Than footprints over a lithograph" (45).

This voice of disillusion about man's life coming to naught is now familiar: it has been Slessor's from the moment he became part of his poetry in the early *Earth-Visitors* period. Was it not behind Heine's question (in "Heine in Paris"): "What now was left of all the passion he'd spilled,/The fire he'd struck?" (13) as it is now behind Dobbin's answer: "no greater a memorial/Than footprints over a lithograph"?

All that is left to Dobbin now is the actual present, and this
is the emphasis in the final stanza, as it was in the first. The
window, the water of the harbor, the ships passing by, and the
retired Dobbin—all are seen again:

> Coldly in the window,
> Like a fog rubbed up and down the glass
> The harbour, bony with mist
> And ropes of water, glittered; and the blind tide
> That crawls it knows not where, nor for what gain,
> Pushed its drowned shoulders against the wheel,
> Against the wheel of the mill.
> Flowers rocked far down
> And white, dead bodies that were anchored there
> In marshes of spent light.
> Blue Funnel, Red Funnel,
> The ships went over them, and bells in engine-rooms
> Cried to their bowels of flaring oil,
> And stokers groaned and sweated with burnt skins,
> Clawed to their shovels.
> But quietly in his room,
> In his little cemetery of sweet essences
> With fond memorial-stones and lines of grace,
> Captain Dobbin went on reading about the sea. (45-46)

Slessor has returned Captain Dobbin to the present, but, in the
last line, he leaves him looking away from it again. Again contemporary life is rejected for the past. This naturally follows,
given Slessor's vision of the present.

The sea in the present outside Dobbin's window has become
burdened with meaning beyond the simple purity and challeng-
ing majesty of itself that Dobbin knew as a young man. Now, in
the harbor, with its "blind tide/That crawls it knows not where,
nor for what gain," and flows over "white dead bodies" below
"in marshes of spent light," the sea is seen not only as death, but
also, in its eternal flow, dumbness, and absence of design, as a
Slessorian view of life itself. This sea of the present outside
the window cannot compete with Dobbin's sea of the past, filled
with "sails bleached with light, salt in the eyes." Nor can those
men who pass today on ships without sails, stokers who "groaned
and sweated with burnt skins,/Clawed to their shovels," compare
with his mates of long ago and the imagined high adventures of

Magellan, Bougainville, and Cook. But for Captain Dobbin, reading and remembering and arranging time into and out of the past is, as has been indicated, finally frustrating and defeating. Now, as an old man, he is left only with a past, and what he seeks, almost unknown to himself, is a stopping of time so that all that was, is, and will be, forever.

V *Slessor's View of Time and the Sea*

Slessor himself seems to wish if not a stopping of time, at least a living outside of it, or some escape from its continuity. Whatever his precise wish, the subject of time, touched upon in several poems, sometimes only in passing as in the early ones, is seen more clearly now as one of his significant preoccupations. But "time" is not the only subject that emerges most vividly as a Slessorian preoccupation in "Captain Dobbin." The "sea" is another, the sea, ever changing as the poet developed, and now a sea fathoms deeper in meaning than the simple waterspouts and bubbling rings recalled from the *Vision* days.[43] Separately and together, the "sea" and "time" become translated in the major poems, beginning with "Captain Dobbin," into a kaleidoscope of ideas and images involving their shifting relationship to each other and their collective and separate relationship to Slessor's dark and persistent vision of man adrift in a life without meaning. Only the vision remains constant: the meanings of sea and time change from poem to poem, from "Captain Dobbin" to "Five Visions of Captain Cook," and from "Five Visions" to the later "Five Bells" and "Beach Burial." And they keep changing as the poems are reread.

The sea is seen as life, but then also as death, and the sea becomes time relentlessly moving man from life into death—beyond which there is nothing. But the sea also is itself, full of beauty and power and exhilarating to the spirit. And time, blending with the tide, is also memory, "the flood that does not flow,"[44] providing man with immortality.

VI *"Five Visions of Captain Cook"*

Slessor's major work, unified by his vision, forms a whole in which each poem illuminates and is illuminated by the other. In *Cuckooz Contrey,* "Captain Dobbin" prepares the reader for the highmindedness and heroism of Cook in "Five Visions . . . ," for Dobbin "worshipped" Cook, that "captain with the sad/And fine white face, who never lost a man/Or flinched a peril" (45). Thus, "Five Visions of Captain Cook" with its sense of mission and mysticism enlarges the significance of Captain Dobbin. The old sailor, recalling the past, is a man as is the great navigator. And if Cook in "Five Visions" drove his ship by his "own blood" and "read fair alphabets in stars," he needed the faith of men like Dobbin to do so, needed their faith and devotion to go with him when he "chose a passage into the dark"—and discovered Australia. Cook ennobles Dobbin and Dobbin humanizes Cook, and both ultimately become Man, Man striving against the sea, which is destiny. Yet, for both, in the end, the effort is futile: Dobbin continues to live, a "lapdog" in a clean shirt, and the conqueror Cook dies, absurdly, killed by an English knife held by a frightened savage, one of a group of "puzzled animals, killing they knew not what/Or why, but killing."

The death of Captain Cook is described in the fifth and final vision of what certainly is not only the best and most original poem in the *Cuckooz Contrey* volume, but also "probably the most important poem for its later influence [on Australian poets] that Slessor has written." Poet Judith Wright reminds us that "Five Visions of Captain Cook" was "the first of many later treatments of the theme of early sea-exploration . . . but no one has treated it either with Slessor's inventive brilliance and lightness, or with his intrinsic melancholy."[45] All five sections (visions) of the poem contribute to this estimate, but none more so than the fifth. "Here at last," poet Chris Wallace-Crabbe testifies, "sharp observations and a fastidious fingering of words are involved in something of the first importance, here as last, Slessor's awareness of life has caught up with his mastery of language."[46]

The actual death of Cook takes only a few lines of the fifth vision. Most of the vison, which constitutes the longest section of the poem, has to do with the present life of Cook's shipmate, Alexander Home, and his remembering of the past, part of which was the killing of his captain. An eternity after the event, Home sees it still in his mind's eye. For though his body now "sat drinking rum in Berwickshire," his eyes "were left floating":

> Half-round the earth, blinking at beaches milked
> By suck-mouth-tides, foaming with ropes of bubbles
> And huge half-moons of surf. Thus it had been
> When Cook was carried on a sailor's back,
> Vengeance in a cocked hat, to claim his price,
> A prince in barter for a longboat.
> And then the trumpery springs of fate—a stone,
> A musket-shot, a round of gunpowder,
> And puzzled animals, killing they knew not what
> Or why, but killing . . . the surge of goatish flanks
> Armoured in feathers, like cruel birds:
> Wild, childish faces, killing; a moment seen,
> Marines with crimson coats and puffs of smoke
> Toppling face-down; and a knife of English iron,
> Forged aboard ship, that had been changed for pigs,
> Given back to Cook between the shoulder-blades.
> There he had dropped, and the old floundering sea,
> The old, fumbling, witless lover-enemy,
> Had taken his breath, last office of salt water. (62)

The death scene is significant to the fifth vision, as it is to the entire poem, but it gains its full power from being part of Home's total memory—his vision—and the contrasting of his present with his past. Yet, simultaneously, Home's vision is dependent upon the four earlier ones for its full impact, as the four are dependent on the fifth; in fact, in the rereading, all the visions, separately and in combination, gain power from each other. The last vision "needs" the previous ones depicting the glory of the live Cook to point up the irony and absurdity of his death. And Home needs them to point up the pathetic quality of his present life so as to contrast it with Cook's past which, by association, is also his own. For, by and large, except for Captain Cook's death and a few beautiful lines, much of Home's past is implied; it is primarily his present which is vividly stated in the fifth vision.

"After the candles had gone out"—so begins the fifth vision and the introduction to Captain Alexander Home. The introduction is different from that accorded Captain Dobbin. There, Dobbin was talked about: "Captain Dobbin, having retired from the South Seas," and so on. Here, a setting is established and Captain Home presented:

> After the candles had gone out, and those
> Who listened had gone out, and a last wave
> Of chimney-haloes caked their smoky rings
> Like fish-scales on the ceiling, a Yellow Sea
> Of swimming circles, the old man,
> Old Captain-in-the-Corner, drank his rum
> With friendly gestures to four chairs. They stood
> Empty, still warm from haunches, with rubbed nails
> And leather glazed like agéd serving-men
> Feeding a king's delight, the sticky, drugged
> Sweet agony of habitual anecdotes,
> But these, his chairs, could bear an old man's tongue,
> Sleep when he slept, be flattering when he woke,
> And wink to hear the same eternal name
> From lips new-dipped in rum.
> "Then Captain Cook,
> I heard him, told them they could go
> If so they chose, but he would get them back,
> Dead or alive, he'd have them,"
> The old man screeched, half-thinking to hear "Cook!" (60-61)

This is Alexander Home, in retirement in a Scottish village, the port that he "had come to with his useless cutlass-wounds/And tales of Cook."

"Cook"—Home's old cronies had been bored away by his endless tales of his captain. And so too had he taxed "Elizabeth, a noble wife but brisk,/Who lived in a present full of kitchen-fumes/And had no past":

> "Cook again! Cook! It's other cooks he'll need,
> Cooks who can bake a dinner out of pence,
> That's what he lives on, talks on, half-a-crown
> A day, and sits there full of Cook.
> Who'd do your cooking now, I'd like to ask,
> If someone didn't grind her bones away?
> But that's the truth, six children and half-a-crown
> A day, and a man gone daft with Cook,"

Home is "gone daft with Cook" because Cook is his past and that is all he has in the present. Elizabeth "had no past" because she could afford only her husband's. Impatient with him, she still knew memories were crucial to him now:

> . . . He had not seen her
> For seven years, being blind, and that of course
> Was why he'd had to strike a deal with chairs,
> Not knowing when those who chafed them had gone to sleep
> or stolen away. . . . (61)

These lines and previous ones engender a sense of pity for Captain Home which, gradually as the poem continues, begins to clothe him with a patheticism more trying on the reader than Dobbin's:

> . . . Darkness and empty chairs,
> This was the port that Alexander Home
> Had come to with his useless cutlass-wounds
> And tales of Cook, and half-a-crown a day—
> This was the creek he'd run his timbers to,
> Where grateful countrymen repaid his wounds
> At half-a-crown a day. . . . (61)

Of course there is more than pity here for Home: there is compassion for him and a sense of indignation, revealed through irony, that a man with such a past should be reduced to such a present. The repeating of "half-a-crown a day" (which picks up Elizabeth's plaint) and the coupling it with "cutlass-wounds" and "grateful countrymen" serves Captain Home well. Yet Slessor wants more from his irony. He would serve Home, but also he would serve all men to whom injustice has been done.

Slessor's concern is ultimately even more encompassing, and the deepening level of his irony reflects this as the poem moves toward its conclusion. If with Home, Slessor calls attention to injustice done to men, with Cook, he calls attention to injustice done to Man. The humble Home is a victim of the indifference of other men: the "grateful countrymen" who repay his wounds "at half-a-crown a day." But the hero Cook is a victim of the indifference of a universe or scheme of things without meaning: "a knife of English iron,/Forged aboard ship, that had been changed for pigs."[47] There is irony present in full measure for the plight of both, but where there is anger at men for hurting Home, there is anguish and bitter laughter at life for killing Cook.

This fifth vision, powerful though it is, could not engage the reader so deeply without the previous four. The poetry of the early visions serves, in effect, to "narcoticize" the reader, so filling him with the glory of Cook, that he is overwhelmed by the revelation of Cook's sudden vulnerability and the final absurdity of his death. In other words, perhaps more precise, Charles Higham says that Slessor "lulls" his readers and places them off-guard, "bewitching them by his rhythms [and] dazzling them by his concrete images into a mental vibration at a submerged plane of thinking." Then, having bewitched his readers, Slessor jolts them into the "shock of discovery [that] all Cook's seeking has ended in blood and death."[48]

In a very real sense, at least in terms of this use of the concrete image and the bewitching effect of his rhythm, Slessor in "Five Visions" is practicing what he has preached. It may be recalled that in his memorable speech before the Australian English Association on "Modern English Poetry" (page 74), Slessor said that "poetry's concern with rhythm" was "its employment as a sort of hypnotic agent which will urge the mind to vibrate at a deeper level of consciousness than that of the superficial world." And, when he spoke of images, Slessor said that the whole structure of English poetry rests on the use of the image: "The choice of the concrete where the abstract would be less racking to the creator, and certainly less searching in its revelation of his power or lack of power."[49] So, too, does Slessor's adaptation of different verse forms for different purposes in each of the visions (blank verse in visions I, II, and V and more traditional stanzas in III and IV) recall and illustrate his remarks (in "Writing Poetry: The How and the Why") about "form"—"that shape of a work . . . which seems most nearly to reflect the shape of emotion which produces it.[50]

From first vision to last, Slessor attempts to fit the form to the feeling, and he does this even within each vision itself. In the final one, for example, the leisurely tempo of Home's remembering of "Beaches wind-glittering with crumbs of gilt,/And birds more scarlet than a duchy's seal/That had come whistling long ago, and far/Away" is suddenly accelerated as these thoughts are blurred by the remembered rush of events leading to Cook's killing. There appears in the verse what poet Wallace-Crabbe calls: "a sense of flexed muscles and abrupt shakes" in which "half-line jolts against half-line, phrase against phrase ['. . .—a stone,/A musket-shot, a round of gunpowder.']." And there is still another change as Cook dies and Home's memory of the event fades. "Peace" Wallace-Crabbe says, "settles down once again, accompanied by the inexorable flow of the sea."[51]

If there is an appropriateness in this falling away and de-acceleration of the rhythm as Cook "falls away" and is *mastered,* so there is equal appropriateness for a strong and surging rhythm when Cook is *master. And* such a rhythm is found in the very first vision when we first meet Cook. Within a few lines, the flowing unimpeded blank verse fills us with a sense of surging adventure as the great Cook sets forth on his voyage of discovery:

> Cook was a captain of the Admiralty
> When sea-captains had the evil eye,
> Or should have, what with beating krakens off
> And casting nativities of ships;
> Cook was a captain of the powder-days
> When captains, you might have said, if you had been
> Fixed by their glittering stare, half-down the side,
> Or gaping at them up companionways,
> Were more like warlocks than a humble man—
> And men were humble then who gazed at them,
> Poor horn-eyed sailors, bullied by devils' fists
> Of wind or water, or the want of both,
> Childlike and trusting, filled with eager trust—
> Cook was a captain of the sailing days
> When sea-captains were kings like this,
> Not cold executives of company-rules
> Cracking their boilers for a dividend
> Or bidding their engineers go wink
> At bells and telegraphs, so plates would hold
> Another pound. Those captains drove their ships
> By their own blood, no laws of schoolbook steam,
> Till yards were sprung, and masts went overboard—
> Daemons in periwigs, doling magic out,
> Who read fair alphabets in stars
> Where humbler men found but a mess of sparks,
> Who steered their crews by mysteries
> And strange, half-dreadful sortilege with books,
> Used medicines that only gods could know
> The sense of, but sailors drank
> In simple faith. That was the captain
> Cook was when he came to the Coral Sea
> And chose a passage into the dark. (57)

This is not the entire vision, but it is sufficient to indicate Slessor's technical and thematic intent. Against the pounding rhythm of the sea, Slessor introduces Cook, identifying him with the old kind of sea captain, in contrast to the modern one and has him make the decision (the choosing of a "passage into the dark") which leads to the discovery and ultimate settling of Australia.

Cook's decision is, of course, crucial for Slessor. "So Cook made choice," he says in the last two lines of the first vision, "so Cook sailed westabout,/So men [like Slessor] write poems in Australia." But seemingly almost as important is Slessor's concern that the reader understands the distinction between the self-sufficient captains of "the powder days" of the past and those of the present who reign by "company-rules" and crack their boilers for "a dividend." Here, as in "Captain Dobbin," Slessor opts for the men of the past, and finally, as the poem continues, for the past itself.

Captain Cook's bold decision to sail westward "into the devil's mouth" (as compared to the more prudent choice of earlier explorers like Bougainville who sailed north with the wind and away from the "dead lee shore") brought him almost flush to the eastern coast of Australia. The short second vision, that of some of Cook's officers, other than Home, is of their faith in Cook and of his masterful handling of his ship along the coast, sailing among islands of the beautiful but treacherous Great Barrier Reef. "They'd sail all day outside a coral hedge" near lovely "water-gardens" of "flowers turned to stone" and "crystal twigs" where reefs were but "a fathom from the keel." They were without fear, though "they slid toward a reef that would have knifed/Their boards to mash, and murdered every man."

> It was the spell
> Of Cook that lulled them, bade them turn below,
> Kick off their sea-boots, puff themselves to sleep,
> Though there were more shoals outside
> Than teeth in a shark's head. Cook snored loudest himself. (58)

But it is not only in *language* that Slessor conveys the confidence of the men in Cook, and of Cook in himself. It is also in the *rhythm* of the second vision, which now no longer surges forward as in the first, but swings easily as the ship sails carefully but confidently among the reefs. Again, in language and rhythm:

> Three officers
> In gilt and buttons, languidly on deck
> Pointed their sextants at the sun. One yawned,
> One held a pencil, one put eye to lens:
> Three very peaceful English mariners
> Taking their sights for longitude
> I've never heard
> Of sailors aching for the longitude
> Of shipwrecks before or since. It was the spell
> Of Cook did this, the phylacteries of Cook.
> Men who ride broomsticks with a mesmerist
> Mock the typhoon. So, too, it was with Cook. (59)

Between the second vision of Cook (that of some of his officers) and the fourth (that of some midshipmen) Slessor pauses, changes the mood, and offers in light rhymed verse an impersonalized view of history. Perhaps "history" is too heavy a word for the delightful play of time measured out by two personalized chronometers in conflict in Cook's cabin. One:

> Arnold choked with appetite to wolf up time,
> Madly round the numerals his hands would climb,
> His cogs rushed over and his wheels ran miles,
> Dragging Captain Cook to the Sandwich Isles.

But the other:

> Kendal dawdled in the tombstoned past,
> With a sentimental prejudice to going fast,
> And he thought very often of a haberdasher's door
> And a yellow-haired boy who would knock no more.

Yet Slessor does intend the chronometers to serve for history: both are made by men and both relate to time. And if the play of the chronometers is amusing, it also becomes unsettling as the relativeness and insignificance of time (and of history) as measured by men become apparent:

> All through the night-time, clock talked to clock,
> In the captain's cabin, tock-tock-tock,
> One ticked fast and one ticked slow,
> And Time went over them a hundred years ago. (59)

In this last line, Slessor allows the reader to cast "Time" as the "Great Enemy." However, he also allows a larger and more significant option in which the eternally flowing Time, though it engulfs Man and all that he creates and hopes for, has no relationship to Man apart from the one that Man himself devises. So seen, Time merges with the general inexplicableness, irrationality, and meaninglessness of the scheme (or the absence of scheme) of things in which Man moves and has being.

Within this context and that of the existential sense of the absurd that will surround Cook's death in the final vision, there is an unexpected poignancy in the light-spiritedness of the fourth vision in which a very human Cook is seen. But this is felt only in retrospect. We take only pleasure in the first reading of this briefest of visions in which the demi-god Cook "descends" to talk shop with his young midshipmen while exploring the shore line of Australia in a small boat. "Sometimes," they recall, "the god would fold his wings/And, stone of Caesars turned to flesh,/Talk of the most important things/That serious-minded midshipmen could wish":

> Of plantains, and the lack of rum
> Or spearing sea-cows—things like this
> That hungry schoolboys, five days dumb,
> In jolly-boats are wonted to discuss.
>
> What midshipman would pause to mourn
> The sun that beat about his ears,
> Or curse the tide, if he could horn
> His fists by tugging on those lumbering oars?
>
> .   .   .   .
>
> Here, in this jolly-boat they graced,
> Were food and freedom, wind and storm,
> While, fowling-piece across his waist,
> Cook mapped the coast, with one eye cocked for game. (60)

At the end of the poem and in the midst of Cook's senseless death we will suddenly remember the "jolly-boat" and the young schoolboy officers and wonder whether they were with Cook when he died and what they felt when their god went down.

And we will remember also "the fowling-piece" and marvel at the innocence of the eye and the vulnerability of the man.

To Slessor, there is nothing particularly hidden or symbolic in "Five Visions of Captain Cook." In fact he sees the entire sequence of poems as "quite straightforward in its intention and expression," one that could be described as "a sort of Identikit likeness, made by superimposing a number of aspects of Cook, seen through the eyes of various men who sailed with him, thus approaching perhaps a total portrait."[52]

At least this is what Slessor wrote in the summer of 1967 in one of his series of five articles in the *Sydney Daily Telegraph* on Australian poetry then being studied in the secondary schools of New South Wales. In the series, which was designed to tie in with the school curriculum, Slessor devoted two of the five articles to his own work, allocating one to a discussion of seven of his poems, including his masterpiece, "Five Bells," and the remaining one to a single poem: "Five Visions of Captain Cook." Slessor says a great deal about the genesis of "Five Visions," responding fully to the article's caption, "Poet tells of the birth of a poem." He acknowledges from the outset that "the whole work owes a great debt to a remarkable man whom I was once privileged to know and visit." This was Captain Francis Bayldon, "a sea-captain himself, if not of the 'powder days' at least of the clipper ship days of the last century." Bayldon, who was the uncle of Slessor's wife, had a "magnificent nautical library" of books, logs, journals, maps and charts which fascinated Slessor on his weekly visits. Equally important was the captain's large enthusiasm, "scholarly gusto and . . . worship of Cook" which soon "infected" Slessor and sent him in pursuit of the great navigator.[53]

Captain Bayldon's library provided the poet not only with information, but also with ideas and images. Captain Home's vision, for example, comes in substance from Home's own manuscript journal, a copy of which Slessor remembers as having "had the good fortune to see." And the fourth vision, that of Cook on a "work-a-day occasion" in a jolly-boat with his young officers, "was derived," Slessor says, "from some verses [discovered in the library] written by one of the midshipmen aboard, later to become Captain Trevenen."[54] Trevenen, like Home, was a member of Cook's company on the third voyage, the voyage of death.

In addition to the genesis of "Five Visions," Slessor devotes much of the *Telegraph* article to an explication of the text, explaining phrases and providing background to subject matter. By and large the explication is helpful. Without it we might not know, for example, that the playful clocks or chronometers of the third vision were supplied by two famous English watchmakers and carried by Cook to test a new method of discovering longitude.[55] Nor might we know that this method is contrasted with the older lunar one, involving complicated calculations, used by the officers in the second vision. We are grateful for the poet's explication; it permits us to participate more deeply in various surfaces of the poem. Yet we leave the article with a sense of having missed something, a sense of having been told a great deal, but of having learned very little of significance. Perhaps this is because "Five Visions" also permits us to take from it much more than Slessor, despite his volubility in the article, indicates that the poem has to offer. Leaving a reading of it, still touched by the wonder of it, the poem seems more to us than Slessor's mechanical "Identikit likeness, made by superimposing a number of aspects of Cook . . . thus approaching a total portrait." Cook dies in Home's memory in the fifth vision, and if Slessor's "portrait" is of Cook alone, the poem should end with the death. But "Five Visions" does not end there; it could not: for the portrait is also of Home. So, in the last stanza, w'.on:

> Cook died. The body of Alexander Home
> Flowed round the world and back again, with eyes
> Marooned already, and came to English coasts,
> The vague ancestral darknesses of home,
> Seeing them faintly through a glass of gold,
> Dim fog-shapes, ghosted like the ribs of trees
> Against his blazing waters and blue air.
> But soon they faded, and there was nothing left,
> Only the sugar-cane and the wild granaries
> Of sand, and palm-trees and the flying blood
> Of cardinal-birds . . .

Blind, penniless on "half-a-crown a day," Home has only the past to sustain him. But finally even this is threatened as the old sailor suddenly appreciates his own mortality and absurdity:

>. . . and putting out one hand
>Tremulously in the direction of the beach,
>He felt a chair in Scotland. And sat down. (62)

These are the last lines and the end of the poem. And it is also Slessor's vision of the end of man. Cook's meaningless death of the past matches Home's pathetic death-in-life of the present, and both are illuminated by the other. This is Slessor's vision, not to be counted as one of the five; the final and ultimate vision embracing all the others and defining and exalting the poem.

In "Five Visions of Captain Cook," as in "Captain Dobbin" and other poems in *Cuckooz Contrey*, Slessor has been the reporter of men's lives, the collector of their visions. He has, in effect, "lived many lives," as he will say in "Five Bells," and in so doing he has served both men, by re-creating them, and his own Muse, by being the true poet, the repository of memory. Simultaneously, Slessor has also significantly served himself as a man, for, in keeping men alive through memory, he has discovered the possibilities of permanence amid the destructive flux and flow of time. And in the reliving of men's lives and visions he has used them to clarify and nourish his own. Certainly, Slessor has done this in "Five Visions" in which, to explain the end of man, he has sought his beginning. Cook, of course, as a figure in history, a symbol for discovery of a country's beginning, and as a man among men, is an ideal subject for re-creation, an ideal "Identikit." The "reporter" Slessor keeps a distance from his subject, at least until the end. Then his anguish breaks through, controlled but overwhelming in the clarity of the vision it projects.

In "Five Bells" this distance will disappear almost entirely, leaving only the anguish and feelings of frustration and helplessness. It will be Slessor's own very personal memories, of a friend long dead, that will inspire his vision. And his admission in the poem that "I have lived many lives" will be a declaration that he no longer has to: that he no longer has to "hide" behind a Heine ("Heine in Paris") nor ransack Captain Bayldon's book to discover Captain Cook. Within the refuge of Sydney Harbor where the "Five Bells" are heard, Slessor's journey of discovery, undertaken as Cook's, with "empty charts," has come to an end. There are no further uses for history and legend and fantasy. Only Slessor remains: to confront his own life and his own death.

CHAPTER 4

The Final Period: 1933-1939
The Poems in Five Bells

"Many hundreds of years ago, in an Arabian fairy tale, a man dipped his head into a basin of magic water. In the few minutes between submerging his face and withdrawing it, he dreamed that he had sailed on seven voyages, was cast up in a shipwreck, captured by pirates, discovered a diamond as big as a turkey's egg, married a princess, fought in many battles, and was brought to execution." So begins Slessor's explanation of his use of time in his masterpiece, "Five Bells." The explanation is part of a second article on his own work that he wrote in 1967 for the *Sydney Daily Telegraph.*[1]

For Slessor, "the point of the [fairy tale] is that although the man's life under water had been a vision, the experiences which he suffered during it . . . were actual as those in his real life." The man in the tale had, in fact, "lived an entire existence on another time scale."

I "*Five Bells*"

This is partly the idea of "Five Bells," the poet tells us, "a poem which suggests that the whole span of a human life can be imagined, and even vicariously experienced in a flash of thought as brief as the interval between the stroke of a bell." So conceived, the poem could be described "as a kind of meditation at night, while looking at Sydney Harbour and hearing the cold fact of time, five bells or half-past 10, rung from a ship at its mooring below."[2] Yet this "cold fact of time" is but one of time's expressions in "Five Bells," for "in the three seconds or so which [the] mechanical process involves, between the double ding-ding and the single ding of the ship's bell, a sequence from a very different time-scale is interposed, compressing about 30

years of human life into the three seconds." It is for this reason,
the poet tells us, that the words "five bells" are repeated throughout the poem: the reader is to be reminded "that time, on the
other scale, has occupied only a few moments, that the tongue
of the bell is still moving and the sound is still suspended in the
air." "Five Bells," therefore, is a two-level poem. "First it attempts to epitomize the life of a specific human being but fundamentally it is an expression of the relativeness of time."[3]

All this is useful information for a full appreciation of the
poem, though, recalling the unrevealed in Slessor's article on
"Five Visions of Captain Cook," we might at first accept it with
some reservations. The first stanza, in fact, might make us wary,
for "time" with which the poem begins, does not at once seem
precisely the kind of time that Slessor has discussed so generously
in his article. "Five Bells" begins a soliloquy, the poet looking out
over the "night and water" of Sydney Harbor:

> *Time that is moved by little fidget wheels*
> *Is not my Time, the flood that does not flow.*
> *Between the double and the single bell*
> *Of a ship's hour, between a round of bells*
> *From the dark warship riding there below,*
> *I have lived many lives, and this one life*
> *Of Joe, long dead, who lives between five bells.* (103)

That which puzzles momentarily at the outset is not Slessor's
philosophical rejection of "time that is moved by little fidget
wheels"—and, by inference, this can be any time able to be
measured by any instrument: the common clock, the special
chronometers carried by Cook, as well as bells. Technically, actually, Slessor is using this aspect of time, as promised in his
article, both stating and demonstrating that the poet's thoughts
come in response to and between "a round of bells/from the dark
warship below."[4]

What is less clear, at least in the first reading, is Slessor's
meaning of and how he intends to use the aspect of time that he
does philosophically accept: "my Time, the flood that does not
flow." Certainly this non-flowing time seems less familiar, if not
almost contradictory to the very character of time to which
Slessor has accustomed us. Certainly, also, such non-flowing

time, would seem difficult to resolve with Slessor's own statement
that "Five Bells" is fundamentally "an expression of the relativeness of time."

All that seems ambiguous, however, gradually recedes as the
poem continues. First, amid the "Deep and dissolving verticals
of light [that] Ferry the falls of moonshine down," and between
the "Five Bells/Colding rung out in a machine's voice," the poet
wonders why thoughts persist "of Joe, long dead," who had
drowned many years before:

> Why do I think of you, dead man, why thieve
> These profitless lodgings from the flukes of thought
> Anchored in Time? You have gone from earth,
> Gone even from the meaning of a name;

No answer comes, only an increasing sense of Joe:

> Yet something's there, yet something forms its lips
> And hits and cries against the ports of space,
> Beating their sides to make its fury heard.

> Are you shouting at me, dead man, squeezing your face
> In agonies of speech on speechless panes?
> Cry louder, beat the windows, bawl your name!

Still no answer, just the bells—intruding upon and creating
thought:

> But I hear nothing, nothing . . . only bells,
> Five bells, the bumpkin calculus of Time.
> Your echoes die, your voice is dowsed by Life,
> There's not a mouth can fly the pygmy strait—
> Nothing except the memory of some bones
> Long shoved away, and sucked away, in mud . . . (103)

Yet, now in the next line, as the poet's thoughts begin to lift Joe
to life, we begin to anticipate an answer:

> And unimportant things you might have done,
> Or once I thought you did; but you forgot,
> And all have now forgotten—looks and words
> And slops of beer; your coat with buttons off,

> Your gaunt chin and pricked eye, and raging tales
> Of Irish kings and English perfidy,
> And dirtier perfidy of publicans
> Groaning to God from Darlinghurst. *Five Bells* (103-104)

Joe is now alive; we can begin to see him. And in the seeing of
him, in the poet's gradual detailing of and response to him in
this and subsequent stanzas, we come to appreciate that, through
Joe, the poet is also reviewing his own life:

> Then I saw the road, I heard the thunder
> Tumble, and felt the talons of the rain
> The night we came to Moorebank in slab-dark,
> So dark you bore no body, had no face,
> But a sheer voice that rattled out of air
> (As now you'd cry if I could break the glass) . . .

Indeed, ultimately we come to appreciate that if the pressure
to remember Joe comes poetically from Joe's shade, seeking
resurrection, it comes no less actually from the older poet's own
yearning to return to his youth and the possibilities of the past.
Even the "speechless panes" of the fourth verse, against which
Joe squeezes his face, seem in retrospect also a mirror reflecting
the anxious face of the older poet looking for his younger self.
There is no question that Joe is recalled to thought by the bells,
but he is fleshed by the intimacy of the poet's knowledge of and
intensity for a past in which Joe had a part. This is revealed in
subsequent verses, and it is our increasing awareness of the
poet's stake in this past that provides the answer to why he is
pressed to remember the dead man. And it is in the fullness of the
poet's remembering: of places, times, and things, of private hopes
and public actions, that the remains of ambiguity disappear.

It is *memory* that is the time frozen between the bells. So conceived, Slessor, poetically, as promised in his article, can compress
in the few seconds "between the double-ding ding and the single
ding of the ship's bell . . . about 30 years of human life."[5] The
poet's "flood that does not flow"[6] is memory; now, finally, of the
poet's own life, no longer, secondhand, that of Cook or Home or
Dobbin, or any other figure salvaged from books and history.
Truly, Slessor had "lived and used many lives"[7] to express his vision. And in this imagined living he has sailed many journeys and

explored many coasts, though, in fact, he seldom ventured far from his room overlooking Sydney Harbor. In a way, Slessor has been like the man in the Arabian fairy tale about whom he talks in his article. He, too, has "dreamed" other lives, but now, growing older and moving toward his own "execution," he has been forced into wakefulness and the use of his own reality to deal with and express his anguished vision of man's plight.

Of course, in "Five Bells," the poet's is still a shared life (with Joe), though now an emotionally actual one, based on his own deeply experienced memories:

> In Sydney, by the spent aquarium-flare
> Of penny gaslight on pink wallpaper,
> We argued about blowing up the world,
> But you were living backward, so each night
> You crept a moment closer to the breast . . . (105)

It is, in fact, the very meaningfulness to the poet, of memory that makes it so vividly the "Flood that does not flow." And the poet is explicit in wanting us to translate memory (time) precisely this way. Later in the poem, after the past has been remembered and Joe is returned to death, the poet calls out after him as he disappears into the atmosphere of the water and bells of the harbor:

> Where have you gone? The tide is over you,
> The turn of midnight water's over you,
> As Time is over you, and mystery,
> And memory, the flood that does not flow . . . (105)

The next-to-last stanza from which these verses are quoted contributes even more significantly to our fuller understanding of the poem. For if the poet's is a shared life in "Five Bells," we do not fully appreciate how deeply shared it is on his part until his sudden outburst of anguish and despair in the final ten lines of the stanza:

> I felt the wet push its black thumb-balls in,
> The night you died, I felt your eardrums crack,
> And the short agony, the longer dream,
> The Nothing that was neither long nor short;

But I was bound, and could not go that way,
But I was blind, and could not feel your hand.
If I could find an answer, could only find
Your meaning, or could say why you were here
Who now are gone, what purpose gave you breath
Or seized it back, might I not hear your voice? (105-106)

It is this later personal expression of pain, in fact, that helps us to reduce the distance that the poet maintains in the earlier stanzas between himself and the "living out" of another's life. Certainly there is less such distance in "Five Bells" than in previous poems, less disguise and more obvious participation by the poet in the life of the man being re-created; after all, "Joe, long dead," was once flesh and blood to the poet. Yet, there remains distance in the earlier "remembering" stanzas, and the poet connects to Joe and is present primarily to the extent that he is needed to resurrect him. That the poet shares deeply in Joe's life, that he has a personal stake in it or the time associated with it, is appreciated largely in restropect. In the first reading the emphasis seems on Joe, it is Joe who matters, his life, and his vision (as before it was only Captain Cook's). In Melbourne it is Joe's anger that "had been leeched away/By the soft archery of summer rains. And the sponge-paws of wetness, the slow damp/ That stuck the leaves of living, snailed the mind" (104). And it is of people close only to Joe of whom the poet writes: "those frames/And shapes of flesh that had perplexed your youth,/And most your father, the old man gone blind./With fingers always round a fiddle's neck,/That graveyard mason whose fair monuments/And tablets cut with dreams of piety/Rest on the bosoms of a thousand men" (105).

After these stanzas, Joe, as has been indicated, is returned to death; time is equated with the memory that had re-created him between the sound of the bells; and the poet—controlled and objective to this point—suddenly breaks and reveals, almost in spite of himself, his very personal concern: "If I could find an answer, could only find/Your meaning . . ." (106).

This is the climax of "Five Bells," among the most telling ones in Australian poetry. The final stanza, which then follows, subdued, expressing weariness and loss of hope, returns the poet to the present where we had first found him, looking out over the "night and water" and listening to "a sound of bells/From the dark warship riding there below":

> I looked out of my window in the dark
> At waves with diamond quills and combs of light
> That arched their mackerel-backs and smacked the sand
> In the moon's drench, that straight enormous glaze,
> And ships far off asleep, and Harbour buoys
> Tossing their fireballs wearily each to each,
> And tried to hear your voice, but all I heard
> Was a boat's whistle, and the scraping squeal
> Of seabirds' voices far away, and bells,
> Five bells. Five bells coldly ringing out. *Five Bells* (106)

II *Background and Interpretations of "Five Bells"*

Though "Five Bells" is the first poem in the *Five Bells*[8] volume, Slessor places it last in his penultimate but definitive[9] collection, *One Hundred Poems*. It is appropriately placed, for "Bells" represents a kind of summing up and bringing together of ideas, themes, and images which have preoccupied Slessor for most of his poetic life since *Earth-Visitors*. "Five Bells" is also, as has been suggested, Slessor's most personal statement. It is not only personal in that he "confesses" his poetic role (his living of "many lives" which ultimately relate to his own), but also in that he is more explicit than ever before in revealing his pent-up feelings about the transitory and isolated nature of man's life and his final separation and disappearance in death.

Certainly, within the context of the poem, it is Joe who seems to trigger these feelings, and in that sense, they "belong" to Joe. But we know also that these are feelings which have been long held by Slessor, and if they are evoked by Joe, they are, at least, no less raised by and are related to other persons, both real ("Burying Friends")[10] and imagined. Joe's drowning in Sydney Harbor nourished Slessor's feelings, but so did Heine's dying in Paris, and Cook's slaughter in the Sandwich Islands.

Of course it is appropriate, indeed part of the poetic tradition, for Slessor to focus his feelings on a friend, "long dead." Yet if we are to receive the intensely personal impact of "Five Bells," we must understand Slessor's feelings as existing also apart from Joe and, in the final analysis, as relating primarily to Slessor himself. That is, it is important to appreciate that Joe, though served by the poet, is also "used" by the poet; that Joe, in effect, is a vehicle for the poet's own most profound and personal feelings. This may be sensed within the context of the poem itself, but is more fully grasped within the wider context of the poet's evolving vision in which each of his important poems relate to, illuminate and are illuminated by, each other.

"Five Bells," so read, does not seem to be quite as elegiac in spirit as most Australian critics suggest. We are less certain, for example, that "Five Bells," in fact "arose," as Douglas Stewart indicates, "in the same way as did Milton's lament for Ned King, Matthew Arnold's for Arthur Hugh Clough and Tennyson's for Hallam."[11] True, it "mourns" (overtly), as do the others, "a friend of the writer's youth." But the impulse for the elegy does not seem to come as forcefully from Joe as from the others, nor do Slessor's emotions seem as intensely or exclusively attached to a single person as are Tennyson's and Arnold's. (Milton's in the incomparable "Lycidas" require a much more elaborate analysis.) Arthur Hallam's death, we know, devastated Tennyson; he withdrew from the world, publishing nothing for ten years, and his later tribute, "In Memoriam," was to his "other self" and represented a needed working-out of a philosophy of life that could accommodate itself to death. Similarly, we know that Arnold, though he and Clough had drifted apart, remained, in "Thyrsis," deeply involved in the philosophical and spiritual conflict that had estranged them. Slessor, both biographically and poetically, seems less directly involved in and less specifically affected by the death of his friend. In fact, as suggested, we are not sure to what extent Slessor's despair is in response to Joe's death and to what extent it is in direct response to his own feelings apart from Joe but for which Joe has been resurrected to serve. In later comments about Joe and about the elegy itself in which he supposedly mourns him, Slessor does not emotionally support the relationship; rather, he seems to depersonalize it.

We are taken aback, for example, when the poet tells us in his *Daily Telegraph* article, that though "Five Bells" attempts "to epitomize the life of a specific human being [Joe], . . . *fundamentally it is* an *expression* of the *relativeness* of *time* [author's italic]." (It must be reminded here that the poet is talking about an elegy to a friend.) Yet, recalling Slessor's natural reserve and penchant for technical discussion and the "how" of poetry, we can accept, though tentatively, this duplication of the impersonal "Identikit of Cook"[12] approach to "Five Bells." However, despite the acceptance, we are still startled by Slessor's subsequent remark that "considered in this light [the poem being an 'expression of the relativeness of time'], the personal allusions are unimportant."[13]

But, of course, the "personal allusions" are important; they are crucial in an elegy, particularly in the most anthologized elegy in Australian poetry. Slessor is very much aware of this, and though he would prefer simply to stay with the poem's purposes and to explicate parts of its text, which he does subsequently, he does appreciate that "a little explanation may be justified" to the many students who "continue to inquire about the identity of Joe and the circumstances of his death." Slessor's explanation is, indeed, "little," and just sufficient to identify "the 'dead man' whose life is re-lived 'between the double and the single bell'." He was:

. . . Joe Lynch . . . a friend of my youth, a black-and-white artist of superb humor and talent whose work appeared in the '20s in many Australian periodicals and who was a member of the staffs of *Smith's Weekly* and *Melbourne Punch* when I, too, worked for them.[14]

This is all that Slessor says about his relationship with Joe, though parenthetically he does add something about Joe's brother, which, in terms of our concern, may seem gratuitous. Yet, the poet's remarks do reveal something of the consistency of his esthetics and possibly something of a nostalgia for the days of his youth, the days of *Vision* and *Earth-Visitors*. He says:

[Joe] was a brother of the sculptor Frank or "Guy" Lynch whose *Satyr* and *Australian Venus* were famous in the '30s. Frank Lynch was old-fashioned enough to believe that sculpture should primarily be a work of beauty rather than of scrap iron and wire, and as a consequence his magnificent *Satyr* now moulders in the cellars of the Art Gallery.[15]

But what about the circumstances of Joe Lynch's death, the death which is mourned in "Five Bells"? Here, too, Slessor's "explanation" is meagre, providing, in effect, little more than the "reporter's" essentials:

One evening in the 1930s, Joe and half a dozen other artists and journalists left Circular Quay by ferry to go to a party on the north side of the Harbor. Joe sat on the lower deck rail of the boat, clad in an ancient tattered raincoat, heavily laden with bottled beer in the pockets. There was a good deal of jollity until someone noticed that Joe had disappeared.

The ferry hove to and there was a wide search, but no trace of Joe Lynch could be found. His body was never recovered and eventually he was presumed drowned.[16]

This, more or less, has been Slessor's response to queries about Joe's death, though, on occasions, he has been even more laconic and removed. A few years earlier in a television interview he said merely that Joe "fell off a ferry-boat and was drowned. Or at least, he was assumed to have drowned. His body was never found, *I believe*" (author's italics). There is, however, a small personal note in the interview that we miss in the article. Speaking of Joe when they first became friends, Slessor says: "I liked his mad Irish humor and his mad Irish rages." The poet then goes on to relate Joe's "madness" to the line in the eighth stanza of the poem when he and Joe "argued about blowing up the world": "I really didn't want to blow up the world, but [Joe] was quite serious about it."[17]

Given Joe Lynch's vitality and madcap qualities. Slessor's account of his death in which he passively disappears into eternity, is certainly less satisfying than that of Philip Lindsay. Phil, a teenager at the time who idolized his older brother, Jack, Slessor's co-editor on *Vision*, and a circle of friends which included the Lynches, recalls Joe's last night in more dramatic terms.

In his autobiography, *I'd Live the Same Life Over*, Phil writes:

Loaded with bottles, [Joe] had been off to some North Shore party with Frank [his sculptor brother], when, tired of the slow progress of the ferry—or, perhaps, of life itself—he had sprung up, saying he'd swim there quicker, and fully dressed, dived overboard. A deckhand had leaped in after him, and lifebelts were thrown. They saw Joe, said Frank, wave cheerily and strike out for Milson's Point; then he vanished in the moonlight. Perhaps a shark got him, or a mermaid— as some said—or the load of bottles in his greasy old raincoat tugged him to the fishes: no one can tell, for the body was never found.[18]

There is a certain zest and charm to Philip Lindsay's account missing in Slessor's. Yet, if the account is more satisfying, emotionally and artistically, it has no larger claim on truth than the poet's. Slessor certainly was aware of Joe's dive overboard, but he chose to limit his account to that which he personally knew of the facts.

Call Slessor's response here more the newspaperman's and less the poet's, or call it another example of the poet's reluctance to romanticize himself or people close to himself. It is, in fact, this affinity for the impersonal and for distance and disguise that makes Slessor's personal note in "Five Bells" so overwhelmingly personal. Whatever the truth, whether Joe, "heavily laden with bottled beer," accidentally fell overboard in Sydney Harbor or deliberately dived overboard, there is a sense of the absurd surrounding his death that is in keeping with Slessor's vision of life.

"Five Bells," as has been indicated, seems the most profound and complete expression of the poet's vision, drawing upon and elaborating the themes, ideas, and images of earlier poems. This is true also, to a certain extent, of the volume itself. For *Five Bells*, even apart from its title poem, includes a sufficient number of other fine poems to allow us to say that it too, in many ways, "represents a culmination of previous work: the climax of a varied but gradual development."[19] One poem, in particular, which contributes significantly to this evaluation, is "Out of Time."

III *"Out of Time"*

Originally the sixth poem in the *Five Bells* volume (1939), "Out of Time," which consists of three sonnets, was placed first by Slessor for his final period (covering poems composed between 1933 and 1939) when he collected his verse for the *One Hundred Poems* book (1944). The original first poem in the 1939 volume, it might be recalled, was the title poem, which Slessor subsequently made his last "summing-up" poem for the 1944 collection. It is instructive to position "Out of Time" as the introductory poem to the final period. So seen, the poem serves as a kind of bridge between the poems of the last volume and those of the earlier ones. "Out of Time" seems not only a culmination or "collecting" of Slessor's previous variations on the theme of time, but, in that it coalesces time with the poet's simultaneous concern with the sea, prepares us for the themes' most sophisticated expression in "Five Bells."

The bitter and beautiful language of the first sonnet, for example, recalls not only the poet's previous images of time as eternally flowing and killing, but, in relating the image to the waves of the Harbor, points to Joe's death in "Five Bells": "The tide is over you . . ./As Time is over you." The sonnet reads:

> I saw Time flowing like the hundred yachts
> That fly behind the daylight, foxed with air;
> Or piercing, like the quince-bright, bitter slats
> Of sun gone thrusting under Harbour's hair.
>
> So Time, the wave, enfolds me in its bed,
> Or Time, the bony knife, it runs me through.
> "Skulker, take heart," I thought my own heart said.
> "The flood, the blade, go by—Time flows, not you!"
>
> Vilely, continuously, stupidly,
> Time takes me, drills me, drives through bone and vein,
> So water bends the seaweeds in the sea,
> The tide goes over, but the weeds remain.
>
> Time, you must cry farewell, take up the track,
> And leave this lovely moment at your back! (88)

Yet the three sonnets of "Out of Time" are most meaningful in terms of themselves. They constitute one of the most poetic of Slessor's poems. If the poet's "quince-bright, bitter slats/Of sun" which pierce the harbor, promise the "Deep and dissolving verticals of light/[that] Ferry the falls of moonshine down" to the water in "Five Bells," it is the intrinsic beauty of the language as language, not simply as a precursor, that is most significant. And it was to the highly poetic essence of the sonnet sequence itself that Slessor's contemporaries responded, to this and to the vitality and sensitivity of the poet. "This man, the most alive of us," Slessor's old *Vision* companion, Hugh McCrae, called him. "This man . . . whose aching songs create sharp joy . . . poet of beauty and cruelty: he has no compeer today."[20]

It is this Slessor, the mature poet committed to beauty and aware of cruelty, who is able to render into a memorable poem what is often a poet's cliché about living out of time. Of course it says a great deal for Slessor's technical competence and art that he is able to sustain through three sonnets a poetic but precise elaboration of an abstraction, while simultaneously involving us very emotionally. Almost unknown to ourselves we are pulled deeper into the poem and carried along by its rhythm and developing image of a single idea. The image evolves naturally from sonnet to sonnet via a bridge of the closing couplet, part of which becomes the opening line of the succeeding sonnet. The final line—"And leave this lovely moment at your back!"—of the first sonnet, for example, leads into the second and provides the impulse for continued development of the image:

> Time leaves the lovely moment at his back,
> Eager to quench and ripen, kiss or kill;
> To-morrow begs him, breathless for his lack,
> Or beauty dead entreats him to be still.
>
> His fate pursues him; he must open doors,
> Or close them, for that pale and faceless host
> Without a flag, whose agony implores
> Birth, to be flesh, or funeral, to be ghost.
>
> Out of all reckoning, out of dark and light,
> Over the edges of dead Nows and Heres,
> Blindly and softly, as a mistress might,
> He keeps appointments with a million years.
>
> I and the moment laugh, and let him go,
> Leaning against his golden undertow. (88)

The pattern is repeated, as part of the couplet of the second sonnet introduces the third:

> Leaning against the golden undertow,
> Backward, I saw the birds begin to climb
> With bodies hailstone-clear, and shadows flow,
> Fixed in a sweet meniscus, out of Time . . . (89)

A couplet closes the third sonnet but simultaneously unifies and brings the whole series together by echoing in its final line the first line of the first sonnet: "The gulls go down, the body dies and rots,/And Time flows past them like a hundred yachts."

What makes "Out of Time" a memorable poem has to do as much with the artist as with his art. It is Slessor, the poet and person, long involved in a dialogue with Time, who is able to combine his feelings with his art to establish a relationship with Time which fully engages us poetically and emotionally. The "Out of Time" sonnets are a "miracle" to poet-critic Max Harris. As has been indicated, personification of an abstraction often leads to a cliché and sterile poetry. But Slessor effects the opposite. "The miracle of these [sonnets]," Harris says, "is that they are devoid of all artificiality. . . . They are not poetic arguments about Time. Time and the experiencing 'I' are expressed in terms of an authentic personal relationship."[21]

IV "Sleep"

An equally memorable poem, perhaps even more of a "miracle" in its almost perfect blend of form and content, is "Sleep," the second poem in both the original *Five Bells* volume and the *One Hundred Poems* collection. In this poem, as in "Out of Time," an abstraction is personified and a personal relationship established, though here the relationship involves an "experiencing you" rather than an "experiencing I," and there is a significant difference in the nature of the experiencing. In "Sleep," we seem to encounter, at first, promises rather than actual experiences—promises by Sleep to the *you* that the *you* will have certain experiences. Yet, simultaneously, because the experiences are promised in splendid poetry they are experienced by the *you* while they are being promised. The first stanza establishes the relationship through which the promiser, Sleep, offers the experiences, and the *you*, the sleeper, accepts them:

> Do you give yourself to me utterly,
> Body and no-body, flesh and no-flesh,
> Not as a fugitive, blindly or bitterly,
> But as a child might, with no other wish?
> *Yes, utterly.*

"Yes, utterly" is lovely, the effortless yielding of the sleeper to Sleep, and the poem may be read with pleasure on this simple level.

But Slessor asks more of his poem. "Sleep," he says:

imagines the nightly human mystery of going to sleep as a surrender to complete selflessness, in the form of a return to the unconsciousness of a child in its mother's body. Thus the nature of sleeping is pictured as the oblivion of pre-life and that of awakening as birth itself.[22]

So imagined, Sleep, the state of unconsciousness, is personified as the mother, and the sleeper, her child. And the child's response to the mother in the first stanza—"Yes, utterly,"—"[is a] consenting to the total immersion of 'body and no-body, flesh and no-flesh' (that is to say, body and mind) within the enveloping ocean of unconsciousness."[23]

Certainly, the poem allows other possibilities of interpretation. Sleep, for example, might be thought of as a woman addressing her lover, and the poem a sexual expression of their love. Of course, also, in that the sexual act relates actually to birth and life and its climax poetically to death, other combinations of meaning present themselves. All these are suggested in Sleep's promises after the sleeper's surrender in the first stanza:

> Then I shall bear you down my estuary,
> Carry you and ferry you to burial mysteriously,
> Take you and receive you,
> Consume you, engulf you,
> In the huge cave, my belly, lave you
> With huger waves continually.
>
> And you shall cling and clamber there
> And slumber there, in the dumb chamber,
> Beat with my blood's beat, hear my heart move
> Blindly in bones that ride above you,
> Delve in my flesh, dissolved and bedded,
> Through viewless valves embodied so—
>
> Till daylight, the expulsion and awakening,
>   The riving and the driving forth,
> Life with remorseless forceps beckoning—
>   Pangs and betrayal of harsh birth. (89-90)

We know Slessor's stated meaning in "Sleep" and, as indicated, the poem permits us to seek additional ones. But with whatever we leave the poem, we are touched with an almost physical awareness that the poet's purpose has been precisely served by the technical devices he has chosen. It may be an exaggeration to say that we, as readers, have been mesmerized by Slessor's blending of idea, sound, and rhythm. It is much less so to suggest that in our reading out loud of Sleep's enticement of the sleeper, we have not escaped the lulling effect of the verse.

How has the poet accomplished this, technically? Essentially, by conducting successfully what he defines as: "an experiment in the narcotic effect of the repetition of certain consonant—structures and vowel sounds . . . the significant vowel-sound [being] the long 'U' in such words and phrases as 'bear you,' 'estuary,' 'carry you,' 'ferry you,' 'take you,' 'receive you,' 'consume you,' 'engulf you,' 'huge cave' and 'huger waves.'"[24] Of course, also, the effect is served by many internal rhymes and assonances such as "ferry" and "burial," "cave," "lave," "waves," "slumber," "dumb," "remorseless," "forceps," and so on.

Reading "Sleep" after having lived out of time and listened to the bells, we discover suggestions or even echoes from the previous poems. Conceptions, as well as actual phrases and individual words, recall a line, for example, like, "So time, the wave, enfolds me in its bed" from "Out of Time." And the state of unconsciousness of sleep, related as it is to pre-life before birth and, by inference, to the absence of life after death, may seem to elaborate on the water imagery of "Five Bells." Also, the comfort of the womb (the past, in terms of returning to it) compared to the discomfort of birth (and the confrontation with the present) reminds us of another preoccupation of the poet.

Yet "Sleep," nothwithstanding its relationship to the other verse, is a unique poem, distinctive unto itself. Even with echoes no poem contributes more to that feeling of "unexpectedness" which poet R. D. FitzGerald found in much of the verse of *Five Bells* where "a new poem is always a new experience." "Sleep" is not the "best" poem in *Five Bells,* as Hugh McCrae would have it, one "which might be bound up with a poem by Donne and not sink,"[25] but it is among Slessor's best verse in what is perhaps his best single collection.

V   *Slessor and McCrae*

McCrae, himself, or rather his poetry, is the subject of another notable poem in the small *Five Bells* volume (only 42 pages and 17 titles). "To the Poetry of Hugh McCrae," with which Slessor originally followed the title poem, is not quite, as "Sleep" is, "a new poem" that provides "a new experience." Rather, it seems an old poem that provides a new experience or even a new poem that offers an old one. Opening stanzas remind us of the *Vision* poems and of "Earth-Visitors" who "once came gusting down/Cloaked in dark furs, with faces grave and sweet . . . /Blown on raven chargers across the world,/For ever smiling sadly in their beards . . .":

> UNCLES who burst on childhood, from the East,
> Blown from air, like bearded ghosts arriving,
> And are, indeed, a kind of guessed-at ghost
> Through mumbled names at dinner-tables moving,
>
> Bearers of parrots, bonfires of blazing stones,
> Their pockets fat with riches out of reason,
> Meerschaum and sharks'-teeth, ropes of China coins,
> And weeds and seeds and berries blowzed with poison—(101)

The "UNCLES" and their coming in the first stanza seem familiar, indeed, as does the excessive piling up of exotic items in the second and the piling up of images in subsequent ones. But the verbal dandy of *Vision* and *Earth-Visitors* has become the consummate artist of *Five Bells,* so the line and the language of the poem are significantly more controlled. Also, if in "McCrae" the poet has a lingering inclination for display, it is much muted by his darkening vision. Thus, even his excessive praise of his friend for enlivening the sterile poetic scene, is offered in heavy terms inharmonious to McCrae who was a singer of joy and delight. Slessor, in effect, burdened by himself, places McCrae in a context that seems too serious and somber for the poet of *Satyrs and Sunlight:*[26]

> So with your boomerangs of rhyme you come,
> With blossoms wrenched from sweet and deadly branches,
> And we, pale Crusoes in the moment's tomb,
> Watch, turn aside, and touch again those riches,
>
> .   .   .   .

Watch, turn aside, and touch with easy faith
Your chest of miracles, but counting nothing,
Or dumbly, that you stole them out of death,
Out of death's pyramids, to prove us breathing.

.   .   .   .

(Look in this harsher glass, and I will show you
The daylight after the darkness, and the morning
After the midnight, and after the night the day
After the year after, terribly returning) . . . (101)

VI *Poems on Friendship*

If we add "To the Poetry of Hugh McCrae" and "Five Bells" to the earlier poems about persons and their work (e.g., Norman Lindsay in "Earth-Visitors," and his etchings in "Realities"), we can see that Slessor's relatively small *oeuvre* includes what are, in effect, several poems of "friendship."[27] This is understandable, not only in terms of Slessor's deep capacity for life and good fellowship, but, more deeply, in terms of the poet's darkened vision of the human condition. In a life lived with the consciousness of death and of the nothingness beyond, man feels alone and isolated, a wandering island.[28] How important it is, then, to have friends! Living with them and, after they die, having memories of them, seem to block, if even momentarily, the flow toward ultimate annihilation. Of course, also, as an Australian, Slessor is touched by the sense of friendship, of "mateship," inherited from the past when men struggled together against the loneliness and the land of the outback; this remains strong in Australia: every man has and is loyal to his "cobbers" and pals. The after-work Australian stampede to the pub, the almost ritualistic gathering of men (no women except barmaids allowed) "shouting" (treating) each other to beers, is, to some extent, an atavistic expression of this feeling of fellowship.

Some of this sense of comraderie and good feeling and lightness of spirit is in another poem, "To a Friend," which, with the exception of "Five Bells," is perhaps one of the best known poems in the volume. Very short (seven quatrains) and very simple and quotable, it is another "tribute" poem, truly sincere but not too serious. The tribute is to "Adam":

> . . . because on the mind's roads
>   Your mouth is always in a hurry,
> Because you know 500 odes
>   And 19 ways to make a curry,
>
> Because you fall in love with words
>   And whistle beauty forth to kiss them,
> And blow the tails from China birds
>   Whilst I continually miss them,
>
> Because you top my angry best
>   At billiards, fugues or pulling corks out,
> And whisk a fritter from its nest
>   Before there's time to hand the forks out,
>
> Because you saw the Romans wink,
>   Because your senses dance to metre,
> Because, no matter what I drink,
>   You'll hold at least another litre . . . (98)

For these reasons and others (e.g., because Adam and he "burn the selfsame flame [that]/No falls of dirty earth may smother"), the poet asks Adam to enlist him in his Abbey of Thélème as a "serving brother."

"To a Friend" is a pleasant poem, but apart from its popularity, it has little importance in Slessor's body of work. The person, to whom the poem is directed, on the other hand, has a larger importance to the poet. Slessor, himself, in an interview, has told us something of Adam's significance for him:

Adam McKay was one of the two men who most impressed me in my years of pupillage. One was Norman Lindsay and the other was Adam McKay. Adam McKay was a newspaperman of a kind which, today, is almost extinct. A man of enormous erudition, great reading, classical knowledge; at the same time, an enormous humour, gusto, fondness for life, eating and drinking and so on. ["To A Friend"] is quite true. It began at one time when Adam McKay said that my generation really knew nothing, that his generation was still much superior and that anything I could do, he could do better. So he began to show me, and he certainly showed me. I think we had a series of contests that lasted all day. We played billiards and he beat me. We played miniature golf—which was a pastime of those days— and he beat me at that. We played a pin game, where you put a

penny in, and he beat me at that. Then he said he could drink four
or five times as much beer as I could hold. We played some music
and he recognized some works of Bach that I certainly hadn't been
able to place—that was the references to the fugues, of course—and
so as you can see, he wiped the floor with me and he proved that he
could do anything I did, better.[29]

VII   *Poems of Sensuous Experience*

That Kenneth Slessor would be attracted to a man like Adam
McKay is easily understood. As suggested earlier, especially in the
chapter on *Cuckooz Contrey,* Slessor, too, is a man of "humor,
gusto, and fondness for life, eating and drinking," with "as huge
an appetite" as the King of Cuckooz Land. That his vision
plagues him with a "sense of overwhelming loss"[30] does not
lessen, in fact, heightens his appreciation of an Adam McKay,
and of men like John Benbow (of "Metempsychosis") and
William Hickey ("The Nabob") who indulge in what physical
life offers and are secure in their passions. Slessor certainly
delights in the things of the senses: of Hickey being "served
by a Rajah in a golden coat/with pigeon-pie . . . Madeira . . .
and Madeira . . . ," or living the life of "Marco Polo" (from
Earth-Visitors), seeing again the "fire-fish in the topaz fount/
with red fins blown like water plants," or stroking once more
the "maces made of beaten brass/And turquoise-hafted sabre-
blades" (8).

Slessor's sensuousness, in fact, often seems to serve him (and
he, it) almost as much as his fine sense of craft. An example
of this is suggested in the poet's apparent pleasure in the
detailing of material things in his verse and the piling up of
sense-evoking images. May not this exercise, too, be linked to
his abiding vision: with the dark and silent nothingness closing
in, should he not grasp at and be comforted by the things that
touch the physical reality of man?

In the poem "Sensuality," Slessor set out to simultaneously
explore and express a blurring kaleidoscope of "experiencing"
involving the senses and the emotions. Originally the next-to-
the last poem in *Five Bells,* Slessor places it immediately after
"Sleep" in the *One Hundred Poems* volume. The shift is understandable. "Sensuality," like "Sleep" seems an experiment in
the direct translation of sense impressions. Unlike "Sleep,"

however, in whose near perfection all traces of experimentation are lost, "Sensuality" *remains* an experiment, an interesting one to be sure, but not wholly successful because we remain too aware of what the poet is attempting to do. Perhaps Slessor's method in this instance is too visible: the coupling of each set of lines by the repetition of its last word, and the continuation of the line, without pause, into the one following it:

> Feeling hunger and cold, feeling
> Food, feeling fire, feeling
> Pity and pain, tasting
> Time in a kiss, tasting
> Anger and tears, touching
> Eyelids with lips, touching
> Plague, touching flesh, knowing
> Blood in the mouth, knowing
> Laughter like flame, holding
> Pickaxe and pen, holding
> Death in the hand, hearing
> Boilers and bells, hearing
> Birds, hearing hail, smelling
> Cedar and sweat, smelling
> Petrol and sea, feeling
> Hunger and cold, feeling
> Food, feeling fire. . . .
> Feeling. (90)[31]

If Slessor, almost from the poems in *Earth-Visitors*, seems to have been a poet with his "pores open," acutely responsive to sensory experiences, the kinds of experience he chooses in "Sensuality" and other poems in *Five Bells* are significantly different from those of the first poems and those of the middle period of *Cuckooz Contrey*. To Professor T. Inglis Moore, in a review, Slessor remains the "sensualist" in *Five Bells*, "the sensualist translating sense impressions into words with a fierce intensity and a delicate precision." But the poet, now also "the intellectualist who has matured into a grim philosopher of time and death," seeks different stimuli. Now his perceptions are realistic excerpts from experience instead of excursions into imaginary worlds. Now he writes of actualities, of "William Street, local trams, and Sydney Harbour, instead of Tartary courts and Cuckooz Contrey."[32]

Certainly a sensualist, as well as a sentimentalist about the actualities of city life, are present in the poem, "William Street." Just sixteen lines, the poem, Slessor tells us, "is a sort of flash-light photograph of the swarming city channel that runs up the hill to King's Cross [akin to Greenwich Village in New York], taken on a rainy night when the surface of the road is coated with a slick of reds and greens and whites reflected from the neon skysigns":[33]

> The red globes of light, the liquor-green,
> The pulsing arrows and the running fire
> Spilt on the stones, go deeper than a stream;
> You find this ugly, I find it lovely.
>
> Ghosts' trousers, like the dangle of hung men,
> In pawnshop-windows, bumping knee by knee,
> But none inside to suffer or condemn;
> You find this ugly, I find it lovely.
>
> Smells rich and rasping, smoke and fat and fish
> And puffs of paraffin that crimp the nose,
> Or grease that blesses onions with a hiss;
> You find it ugly, I find it lovely.
>
> The dips and molls, with flip and shiny gaze
> (Death at their elbows, hunger at their heels)
> Ranging the pavements of their pasturage;
> You find it ugly, I find it lovely. (99)

Obviously, Slessor sought and achieved more than a flat "flash-light photograph" of William Street. He attempted, he says, "to create [its very] neon-lit, metallic and floozy atmosphere." How? By "the deliberate use of assonance—the kind of asson-ance used not so deliberately in the vulgar old comic songs which still delight me . . . I have rhymed in this way such words as 'green' and 'stream,' and 'men' and 'condemn'."[34]

Today, thirty years after Slessor first published "William Street," the street still exists but the "atmosphere" that had excited his senses has changed. "There have been inexorable changes since the poem was written," he says. "The old fish-shops and '21 meals for £1' cafés have given way to pizza-counters and American hamburger bars and second-hand clothes no longer hang in pawn-shop windows." Yet, he says, and this seems meaningful: "the general reason for the poem remains, since it was intended as a defence of metropolitan fascination against those who considered the city "ugly" and found beauty only in the outback."[35]

Slessor was among the first to deal in his poetry with the life of the city. In fact, Australian literature, as a whole, seems very late in coming to terms with the urban setting. The novel, for example, until well into the thirties, remained preoccupied almost entirely with the outback—and this at a time when the vast majority of the population was already concentrated in towns and cities (see Chapter 1). Indeed it is fair to say that when Slessor wrote "William Street" and other "city" poems, the outback was still idealized by most Australians, and most identified themselves with an image of the outback "Aussie," tough, irreverent of authority, mildly ironical, and always loyal to his mates. When therefore, Slessor says that the "reason for the poem remains," can we not infer, in part, that these old ideas and feelings are still present in contemporary life? Certainly they were present to some extent as late as 1950 when newspapers still spoke of "the real, typical Australian [as living] outside the capital cities."[36]

Whatever their current status, the over-all persistence of these almost atavistic feelings for the Australian bush is a subject worthy of discussion in connection with a people who are among the most tough-minded and pragmatic in the world. Slessor, himself the urban sophisticate wryly critical of the idealization of country life, has nevertheless been touched deeply by the landscape and the life away from the teeming cities. The "Smoulders of puffed earth/And pebbles and shell-bodied flies" in the "aching valley"[37] of Talbingo River are not "lovely" for him as are "the red globes of light" and "the pulsing arrows" of William Street or his waking at five, to "rise, rub on the smoking pane/A port to see,"[38] but he does not forget them. Nor does he forget the silence and sterility of the "straw-coned country" where "the sky lies empty" and "the sun is as white as moonlight,"[39] and the "crow-countries graped with dung" and "gullies that no longer flow/And wells that nobody can find."[40] A Sydney man, these away-from-Sydney experiences have been very meaningful to the poet as have been his memories of country towns, with "willows and squares,/And farmers bouncing on barrel mares."[41]

In *Five Bells,* Slessor further explores the rural area, moving in two directions along the coast, north and south from Sydney. The poems "North Country" and "South Country" are placed together in both the original volume and in *One Hundred Poems,* for Slessor intends a contrast between "the densely timbered forests of the north and the bare, rolling cattle-grazing hills of the south."[42] Both fine poems in their own right, they balance each other and successfully secure Slessor's contrast. Seen first is the "North Country, filled with gesturing wood,/With trees that fence, like archers' volleys,/The flanks of hidden valleys/Where nothing's left to hide:

> But verticals and perpendiculars,
> Like rain gone wooden, fixed in falling,
> Or fingers blindly feeling
> For what nobody cares;
>
> Or trunks of pewter, bangled by greedy death,
> Stuck with black staghorns, quietly sucking,
> And trees whose boughs go seeking,
> And trees like broken teeth
>
> With smoky antlers broken in the sky;
> Or trunks that lie grotesquely rigid,
> Like bodies blank and wretched
> After a fool's battue . . . (93)

Then, striking out in the opposite direction from Sydney, high above the sea but looking inland: "After the whey-faced anonymity/Of river-gums and scribbly-gums and bush,/After the rubbing and the hit of brush,/You come to the South Country":

> And over the flat earth of empty farms
> The monstrous continent of air floats back
> Coloured with rotting sunlight and the black,
> Bruised flesh of thunderstorms:
>
> Air arched, enormous, pounding the bony ridge,
> Ditches and hutches, with a drench of light,

> So huge, from such infinites of height,
> You walk on the sky's beach
>
> While even the dwindled hills are small and bare,
> As if, rebellious, buried, pitiful,
> Something below pushed up a knob of skull,
> Feeling its way to air. (94)

These are memorable poems, indicating again how deeply the urban Slessor responds to the landscape. "South Country," in particular, seems a very personal poem, though always, as in his best poems, the poet's involvement is restrained and unsentimental—Slessor is part of the scene he is describing and yet apart from it, and the fact of his apartness adds force to his presence.

A kind of restraint is also evident in the nature of the imagery the poet uses to translate the landscape. He does not indulge himself in forceful personification and chance the sentimental cliché. Rather, he resorts to what R. G. Howarth called "semi-animation" in which:

. . . natural objects are endued with half-life: the river-gums have, as it were, white unfeatured faces, the brush is able to rub and strike you as you pass, the trees argue, doubt, quarrel, plot, take pains together; the thunderstorm bruises; the small bare hills resemble protruding skulls of living creatures underground. The "monstrous continent of air," too, is almost animated, given life—it arches, it rains blows of light on the ridge. Personification would be too gross: Slessor suggests, half-uncovers, gives just enough for the purpose.[43]

A similar restraint and indefiniteness in Slessor's use of sound in the poem is also demonstrated:

Thus part-rhyme runs throughout: "anonymity-country"; "bush-brush"; "done-solution"; "farms-storms"; "ridge-beach"; "pitiful-skull"; with an interposition of rhyme in the two successive middle lines of each set of four, reversed in the last set to bring the part-rhymes into succession medially. Other part-rhymes occur internally: e.g., "ditches-hutches," and assonance and consonance, including the part-rhymes and rhymes, wind throughout: "whey-faced"; "anonymity," "river," "scribbly," "hit"; "gums," "rubbing," "brush," "country," "done"; "plots," "pains," "planes," and so on.[44]

The climax of "South Country," the vision of "the sky's beach," achieved by this imaginative and skillful use of sound in harmony with imagery, is one of Slessor's more beautiful and liberating visions. Such a vision, which allows the the spirit to soar, is rare among the remaining poems in the volume. None of the poems, however, escape the poet's awareness of the end of man and the void beyond or his reflections of despair and disillusionment.

In "Last Trams," people pass through life "Filled with dumb-presences/Lobbed over mattresses,/Lusts and repentences,/Ardours and solaces,/Passions and hatreds/And love in brass bedsteads." Traveling on trams, they look out on this life (their life) "Lost now in emptiness" and are themselves looked at through lighted windows, as they pass:

> Like phantoms in the window-chink,
> Their faces brush you as they fly,
> Fixed in the shutters of a blink;
>
> But whose they are, intent on what,
> Who knows? They rattle into void,
> Stars of a film without a plot,
> Snippings of idiot celluloid. (95-96)

"Who knows?" The poet knows, in his nihilism, and knowing, he would grasp the moment, for there is no other. He tells this to "Lesbia's Daughter" who might be content with words and bloodless men who would "embalm [her] beauty . . ./In boastful odes . . . ." The poet "a more honest man," advises her to live now, for:

> Where's the fine music that the fossil men
> Of lost Lemuria brandished on a pen?
> All tossed in earth—men, music, lovers gone—
> And where's the lust a skull has for a bone?
>
> If joy can turn a moment to a year,
> Why take to Then and There what's meant for Here,
> Or nurture for a cemetery tense
> The curious pleasures of impermanence?

> Look for no lovers on that later scene,
> Let it avail you Are, who shall have Been,
> Burnt utterly the stick you had to burn,
> Lived once, loved well, gave thanks, and won't return. (91)

In "The Vesper-Song of the Reverend Samuel Marsden" no one has to advise the lusty reverend to take pleasure in the day. He is a man with full senses, like William Hickey (in "The Nabob") and John Benbow (in "Metempsychosis"). But the good reverend has special and unique tastes; he delights in the flogging of sinners:

> My cure of souls, my cage of brutes,
> Go lick and learn at these my boots!
> When tainted highways tear a hole,
> I bid my cobbler welt the sole.
> O, ye that wear the boots of Hell,
> Shall I not welt a soul as well?
> > O, souls that leak with holes of sin,
> > Shall I not let God's leather in,
> > Or hit with sacramental knout
> > Your twice-convicted vileness out? (97)

And so faithful is the Reverend Marsden in his efforts to "let God's leather in" that when he hopes for a hereafter, the hereafter is Hell "where [with a whip] blood is not so hard to fetch." Of course, all that he does or hopes to do (his pleasures, his cruelty, and sadism) is for the glory of God:

> Lord, I have sung with ceaseless lips
> A tinker's litany of whips,
> Have graved another Testament
> On backs bowed down and bodies bent.
> My stripes of jewelled blood repeat
> A scarlet Grace for holy meat.
> > Not mine, the Hand that writes the weal
> > On this, my vellum of puffed veal,
> > Not mine, the glory that endures,
> > But Yours, dear God, entirely Yours. (97)

In this "Vesper-Song" Slessor is passing judgment against the lash-hungry chaplain of the convict colony at New South Wales

who blocked efforts in the early nineteenth century to make
life more tolerable for the convicts and freedmen. Flogging
was a savage punishment which had a noxious effect on the
morale of the colony and on the development of the country.
As historian Manning Clark has pointed out:

The unflogged man believed in his future; the flogged man generally
surrendered to despair and moved from one wretchedness to another
till he ended his days at a "launching into eternity" ceremony, or
took to the bush, where he lived like a savage.[45]

Yet if Slessor is passing judgment against the man, Marsden,
he no less is speaking against that which Marsden stood for:
self-righteousness, hypocrisy, intolerance, lack of charity and
compassion.

In the larger context of the poet's work, the qualities given
Marsden are seen as belonging to many men. Many men, even
without whips, have whipped their fellows, hurting them, de-
humanizing them, lessening them. This is the way it has been;
this is the way it increasingly is. Few men, in fact, even good
men, will not at some time in the name of some God, goal, or
idol buy something on the "Cannibal Street" of modern life.
And no man ultimately will escape from being sold there. " 'Buy,
who'll buy,' the pedlar sings" along "Cannibal Street":

> "Bones of beggars, loins of kings,
> Ribs of murder, haunch of hate,
> And Beauty's head on a butcher's plate!"
>
> Hook by hook, on steaming stalls,
> The hero hangs, the harlot sprawls;
> For Helen's flesh, in such a street,
> Is only a kind of dearer meat.
>
> "Buy, who'll buy," the pedlar begs,
> "Angel-wings and lady-legs,
> Tender bits and dainty parts—
> Buy, who'll buy my skewered hearts?"
>
> Buy, who'll buy? The cleavers fall,
> The dead men creak, the live men call,
> And I (God save me) bargained there,
> Paid my pennies and ate my share. (100)

"Cannibal Street" closes the *Five Bells* volume on a note of disillusionment, despair, and disgust. That Slessor chose to end on this note was not inappropriate for the time, though whatever the poet's intention it had nothing to do with the fact that *Five Bells* was to be his last book of new poems; this was not known in 1939. "Cannibal Street" and its ending note now seem, in retrospect, to have been, at least in part, a response to—and a pause of anguish before—the horror of the world war then beginning to close in.

But if Slessor's first ordering of the *Five Bells* poems in 1939 was not inappropriate, so much more felicitous was his rearrangement of them in 1944 for the *One Hundred Poems* volume, which incorporated the three previous collections, *Earth-Visitors, Cuckooz Contrey,* and *Five Bells.* By this rearrangement, "Five Bells" became, in effect, the closing poem if not also the climactic poem of Slessor's complete body of work. This was an act of creative "editing." As indicated, the ideas, images and themes echoing in "Five Bells" were those which seemed to have governed Slessor's poetic life. Also, more than any other poem, "Five Bells" seemed to have expressed most successfully that which the poet had sought to accomplish in his "experiments" in rhyme and in his search for a "form" that would most nearly "reflect the shape of the emotion which produced it." Surely, "Five Bells" had the scope, the tone, the restraint, and the encompassing dignity to be the capstone of Slessor's poetic career.

These are some of the considerations which probably guided the poet in his shifting of "Five Bells" in 1944. Still another one, possibly equally significant, might be added. This had to do with the experiences of the war from which Slessor had just returned. After four years of combat service as Official Australian War Correspondent, the poet knew more than ever before the self-destructiveness and sense of absurdity attached to modern man's living and dying. "Disillusionment," "despair" —these were now felt even more strongly. But "disgust," the disgust of "Cannibal Street"—this would not serve the men he had known, the men he had seen die on the sands of the Western Desert of Egypt and in the lush jungles of eastern New Guinea. "Disgust," yes, at death, but not at their dying; in the heat and horror of their passing, they were deserving only of honor, and honor required a sense of dignity. "Five Bells" with its ultimate pity and restraint would serve them.

Of course, in serving the men, Slessor was also serving himself. For in the knelling of the bells, blended with the living and dying and disappearance of man, did Slessor not sense the farewell statement for himself as a poet? And could not "Five Bells" serve him, the war correspondent, as a sort of final "dispatch" from the front to the relatives of the fighting men who had read and reread his dispatches throughout four years of war? Yet, very soon afterwards, there was to be a short but beautiful postscript, a poem conceived at the scene of battle and written for the men who had died, but also, in a larger sense, for those who had lived, who still had the opportunity to live better. This was "Beach Burial."

VIII *Postscript*

"Beach Burial" was published within a year of *One Hundred Poems* and immediately became an anthology piece, appearing in *Poetry in Australia 1945*. This was its first anthology publication; there were to be many more, as gradually the poem became perhaps the most meaningful one to emerge from the war. Slessor collected "Beach Burial" in 1957 when he finally added it to the *One Hundred Poems* volume, including along with it two other short poems, "Polarities," about the attraction and repulsion of lovers, and "An Inscription for Dog River," about the death and lost identity of soldiers and their vainglorious general. With the addition of these poems and "Beach Burial," *One Hundred Poems* was retitled *Poems* and became the definitive collection. And in that collection, which remains unchanged today, "Beach Burial" became the last poem and its twenty lines a beautiful postscript.

The time of "Beach Burial" is 1942 when the Australians were fighting in the Egyptian desert near El Alamein and the German advance had been stopped. The setting is the beach along the Mediterranean coast where the Germans were encamped. "In the morning," the poet remembers, "it was not uncommon to find the bodies of drowned men washed up on the beaches. They were buried in the sandhills under improvised crosses, identification usually being impossible. Most of them were sailors, some British, some German or Italian, some of them 'neutrals'."[46]

Both in terms of time and setting all this seems an eternity removed from Sydney of the middle thirties, the poet sitting in his room overlooking the harbor, and hearing from below a ship's bell knelling out the hour. There are no bells, as such, in "Beach Burial," only "the sob and clubbing of the gunfire." Yet we might imagine bells, for there are things in this brief, muted elegy that recall the earlier poem, that, in effect, make it a kind of postscript to it:

> Softly and humbly to the Gulf of Arabs
> The convoys of dead sailors come;
> At night they sway and wander in the waters far under,
> But morning rolls them in the foam.
>
> Between the sob and clubbing of the gunfire
> Someone, it seems, has time for this,
> To pluck them from the shallows and bury them in burrows
> And tread the sand upon their nakedness;
>
> And each cross, the driven stake of tidewood,
> Bears the last signature of men,
> Written with such perplexity, with such bewildered pity,
> The words choke as they begin—
>
> *"Unknown seaman"*—the ghostly pencil
> Wavers and fades, the purple drips,
> The breath of the wet season has washed their inscriptions
> As blue as drowned men's lips,
>
> Dead seamen, gone in search of the same landfall,
> Whether as enemies they fought,
> Or fought with us, or neither; the sand joins them together,
> Enlisted on the other front.
>
> *El Alamein.* (109)

The sea, the tide, the death by drowning, the common end of man, his loss of identity and ultimate anonymity—these are echoes from "Five Bells." But if "Beach Burial" is a "P.S.," it is an exceedingly significant one. In just twenty lines, among his purest and most perfect, Slessor moves beyond despair to hope and purpose. Men must die and disappear, yes, even when "plucked" from the watery land of the dead and buried on shore, their anonymity proclaimed: *"Unknown seaman."* Yet the fact that men must die, friend and foe alike, is the reason that men should live together in peace, should be united in life as ultimately they will be united in death. For, if in life, "as enemies they fought," in death, "the sand joins them together,/Enlisted on the other front."

This "other front," the poet tells us, is "the common front of humanity's existence," and

all men of all races, whether they fight with each other or not, are engaged together on [this front]. . . . The absolute fact of death unites them. Their hatreds, quarrels and war should be dwarfed by the huger human struggle to survive against disease and cataclysm on this dangerous planet.[47]

This is, perhaps, the note on which to end our discussion, for though in prose, these comments reflect the poet's concern and "simple earnestness" with which he has spoken "to common men and women" all his life. There is, in fact, an appropriateness that these last remarks are in prose, for Slessor's is no longer a *poetic* voice, though a very active and deeply involved one in behalf of poetry and its relationship to the values by which men live and die. It is felicitious, too, that these comments are addressed to students, for the youth of Australia are important to the poet. His verse, completed over a quarter of a century before they were born, has touched them, and he, in turn, has been touched by their response to it. But the art and revelation of Slessor's poems are timeless in their appeal, and, increasingly, the older reader, as well as the young one, is rediscovering or discovering for the first time, their power, precision, and delicacy.

Notes and References

General

All quotations from Kenneth Slessor's poetry are from *Poems* (Sirius edition, 1964), and numbers in parentheses placed beside quoted verse refer to pages in this volume. Pages mentioned within the text of Chapter 2 refer specifically to the magazines or separate collections under discussion.

Published by Angus and Robertson of Sydney, Australia, *Poems* is not generally available in the United States, though copies of it or an earlier collection, *One Hundred Poems*, can be found at major public and university libraries. Of course, also, copies are available at the libraries of the various Australian Consulate Offices. In addition, *Poems* may be obtained from the publisher's distributor in the United States: Tri-Ocean Books of San Francisco, California.

Preface

Two paragraphs from the preface originally were published by the author as part of "Out of the Oldest Continent," a review of the definitive two-volume collection, *Poetry in Australia,* which appeared in the Summer 1965 issue of *The Kenyon Review.*

Chapter One

1. A phrase used by literary and social critic A. A. Phillips in his article, "The Cultural Cringe," *Meanjin,* IV, 1950, to describe a sense of inferiority felt by Australian writers and artists when faced with "the intimidating mass of Anglo-Saxon culture." (*Meanjin,* a quarterly, has long been edited by C. B. Christesen at Melbourne University.)

2. From "Thieves Kitchen," an early poem, composed between 1919 and 1926. Gallipoli was the site of a heroic defeat by the Australian-New Zealand forces during World War I. Anzac Day, April 25, commemorating the event, is, perhaps, Australia's most important holiday.

3. Charles Higham, "The Poetry of Kenneth Slessor," *Quadrant,* December, 1959, p. 65. *(Quadrant,* published every other month from Sydney, is sponsored by the Australian Committee for Cultural Freedom and edited by author Donald Horne and poet James McAuley, Professor of English, University of Tasmania.)

4. From "Five Visions of Captain Cook," a poem composed during Slessor's middle period, 1927-1932.

5. From "William Street," a poem composed during Slessor's third phase, 1933-1939.

6. From sequence IV in the twelve-sequence "Music" poem, which bridges Slessor's early and middle periods.

7. Originally published by Pellegrini & Cudahy, 1949, in New York; now a Mentor Book, published by the New American Library in New York.

8. Charles Higham, p. 65.

9. "English Project 3," *Sydney Daily Telegraph,* Monday, July 24, 1967, p. 16, col. 1.

10. Vincent Buckley, "Kenneth Slessor: Realist or Romantic?," *Essays in Poetry, Mainly Australian* (Melbourne: Melbourne University Press, 1957), p. 121.

11. Chris Wallace-Crabbe, "Kenneth Slessor and the Powers of Language," *The Literature of Australia,* ed. Geoffrey Dutton (Ringwood, Victoria, Australia, 1964), p. 352.

12. Max Harris, *Kenneth Slessor, Australian Writers and Their Work,* ed. Geoffrey Dutton (Melbourne, 1963), p. 42. This is a 48-page pamphlet.

13. Max Harris, *Kenneth Slessor,* cited by author, p. 5.

14. George Blaikie, *Remember Smith's Weekly* (Adelaide, 1966), p. 49.

15. Kenneth Slessor, "Writing Poetry: The Why and the How," *Southerly,* 3 (1948), 171. This is a text of an Australian Broadcasting Commission broadcast. *(Southerly,* a quarterly, publication of the Sydney branch of the Australian English Association. Editors have included Slessor; more recent ones have been associated with Sydney University.)

16. In a television interview with John Thompson, "Poetry in Australia—Kenneth Slessor," the text of which was printed in *Southerly,* 3 (1966), the poet recalls, "My first printed work was published by *The Bulletin* when I was about fifteen years old" (p. 190).

17. Jack Lindsay, *The Roaring Twenties* (London, 1960), p. 55.

18. *Ibid.,* p. 55.

19. *Vision* (A Literary Quarterly), I (May, 1923), Foreword, p. 2.

20. Interview with John Thompson, p. 191.

21. George Blaikie, p. 130.

22. Jack Lindsay, p. 238.

23. T. Inglis Moore, "Kenneth Slessor," *Southerly*, 4 (1947), p. 194.

24. H. M. Green, *A History of Australian Literature* (Sydney, 1961), Vol. II, p. 856.

25. Jack Lindsay, p. 96.

26. Nettie Palmer, *Modern Australian Literature, 1900-1923* (Melbourne, 1924), The Lothian Prize Essay dealing with "Vision" movement, p. 57.

27. From "The Bush," by Bernard O'Dowd (1866-1953), the radical and political "Poet Militant" of Melbourne who spoke for a poetry of purpose. *The Poems of Bernard O'Dowd* are published by Lothian Publishing Company of Melbourne. A paperback selection by A. A. Phillips is published by Angus and Robertson.

28. In the order quoted, the three quotations are from "Earth-Visitors" (p. 1), "Rubens' Innocents" (p. 7), and "Taoist" (p. 6) in *Poems*.

29. Clement Semmler, *Kenneth Slessor, Writers and Their Work: No. 194*, ed. Geoffrey Bullough, (London, 1966), p. 14. This is a 44-page pamphlet.

30. H. M. Green, *Modern Australian Poetry* (Melbourne: Melbourne University Press, 1946), introductory to first edition, p. VII.

31. Douglas Stewart, *Poetry in Australia*, II, *Modern Australian Verse*, (Berkeley and Los Angeles: University of California Press, 1964), introduction, p. XXX. First published by Angus & Robertson of Sydney, Australia, 1964.

32. Vincent Buckley, p. 118.

33. Douglas Stewart, p. XXX.

34. Quoted in the *Melbourne Herald*, February 24, 1944.

35. Notes 11, 12, and 29 refer to some literary examples. Bibliography includes more general ones.

36. Edited by Colin Thiele and Ian Mudie and published in Adelaide, 1961.

37. Poet Thomas Shapcott, in a letter, "Slessor's Poetry," in *The Bulletin* (January 28, 1957), p. 17. (*The Bulletin*, of Sydney, particularly through its "Red Page," played an important part in shaping Australian literature at the turn of the century and during the early years of nationhood.)

38. See notes 8 and 23.

39. Vance Palmer, *The Legend of the Nineties* (Melbourne: Melbourne University Press, 1954), p. 57. Palmer is expressing the point of view of G. B. Barton, Australia's first serious literary critic (see note 57). Palmer had opened Chapter 3 of *Legend* (Myth-Making) with: "It has been said that men cannot feel really at home

in any environment until they have transformed the national shapes around them by infusing them with myth."

40. From "Shearers," one of many ballads by Henry Lawson (1867-1922), a contemporary of Paterson and a major figure in Australian literature primarily because of his superb stories and prose sketches.

41. From "Saltbush Bill," a ballad by A. B. (Banjo) Paterson (1864-1941).

42. From "Waltzing Matilda," a ballad by Paterson, as are "Clancy of the Overflow," "The Man from Snowy River," and "The Man from Ironbark." (All the ballad quotations are from *Poetry in Australia*, vol. I, *From the Ballads to Brennan*, edited and with an introduction by T. Inglis Moore. See note 31.)

43. This is from a quotation in Vance Palmer, *National Portraits* (Sydney, 1940), p. 125, cited by R. M. Crawford, *An Australian Perspective* (Madison: The University of Wisconsin Press, 1960), p. 36.

44. R. M. Crawford, *An Australian Perspective*, p. 36.

45. Nettie Palmer, p. 57.

46. "Farewell to Old England," Anonymous, is a version of one of the street ballads about transportation (exile) to the convict colony of "Botany Bay". (New South Wales) that survived in oral tradition. This and other similar early ballads are included in *Poetry in Australia*, I, cited in notes 31 and 42. However, more accessible to the American student is the paperback, *The Penguin Book of Australian Ballads* (1964), edited by Russel Ward. The book includes an informative introduction. More interested readers are referred to Douglas Stewart's and Nancy Keesing's *Old Bush Songs and Australian Bush Ballads* published by Angus and Robertson, Sydney, 1955.

47. Russel Ward, *Australia* (Englewood Cliffs, New Jersey, 1965), p. 20.

48. Judith Wright, "Inheritance and Discovery in Australian Poetry," *Literary Australia* (Melbourne, 1966), p. 2.

49. As New South Wales grew from being a convict settlement to a colony, the British Crown began to encourage migration of men of capital and genteel birth. They "assisted" them with large grants of land, use of convict labor, and so on.

50. A chorus from "The Settler's Lament," anonymous (see note 46 re: *Poetry in Australia*). Henry Kendall (1839-1882), one of Australia's first serious imaginative poets, was born in the Ulladulla district on the South Coast of New South Wales.

51. T. Inglis Moore, *Poetry in Australia*, I, *From the Ballads to Brennan* (Berkeley and Los Angeles: University of California Press, 1964), in introduction, pp. xxx-xxxi.

52. *Ibid,* pp. xxx-xxxi.

53. An excellent collection is *Selected Poems of Henry Kendall,* selected, with biographical and critical introduction and a bibliography, by T. Inglis Moore, and published in Sydney, 1957. A paperback edition for students is available from Angus and Robertson or their distributor in the United States: Tri-Ocean Books of San Francisco.

54. Kenneth Slessor, "Australian Literature," *Southerly,* 1 (1945), p. 33.

55. *Ibid.,* p. 31.

56. Kenneth Slessor, "Australian Authors Reply," *Australian Letters,* I, 1 (June, 1957), p. 18. In this quarterly of Australian writing and criticism, a group of Australian poets, including Slessor, was asked to reply to English critics who had commented on some volumes of Australian poetry. (*Australian Letters* is edited by Max Harris, Geoffrey Dutton and others at Adelaide.)

57. G. B. Barton, *Poets and Prose Writers of New South Wales* (Sydney, 1866), pp. 193-94. (Cited by John Pengwerne Matthews, *Tradition in Exile* [Melbourne, 1962], p. 79.)

58. "Australian Literature (no. III), Charles Harpur," *Colonial Monthly* (February, 1869), p. 448. (Cited by Matthews, p. 59.)

59. *Australian Letters,* p. 18.

60. H. M. Green, *Australian Literature,* 1900-1950 (Melbourne: Melbourne University Press, 1951), p. 13. If the Australian contemporary poet winces at his representative at Westminster, so may the American. For if Gordon earned his bust for the ballads and the galloping rhymes, so Longfellow earned his for the blacksmith and the galloping ride of Paul Revere. Similarly, as Poe was not indigenous, and an indigenous Whitman too wild to be "pigeonholed" and honored, so neither could Australia's greatest poet before Slessor, Mallarmé-inspired Christopher Brennan (1870-1932), whose verse reflects none of the "Australianism" of the time.

61. Cited in Jack Lindsay, *The Roaring Twenties,* p. 90.

62. A popular school of verse-writers, among the best of whom were James Brunton Stephens ("The Dominion of Australia") and Essex Evans ("Ode for Commonwealth Day"). Both patriotic men, their poems, conventional and Tennysonian, were admired when published, though they are now more or less (and deservedly so) forgotten.

63. Jack Lindsay, *The Roaring Twenties,* p. 226.

64. Poet Rex Ingamells (1913-1955), a leading figure in the movement and editor of *The Jindyworobak Anthology,* first used the word "Jindyworobak" in a little magazine, *Chapbook,* published in Adelaide, 1935-36, which included poems incorporating aboriginal

words. Ingamells said: "Jindyworobak is an aboriginal word which means to annex, to join. It should appropriately indicate what I have tried to do in the poems published here: namely, to express something of the Australian place spirit which baffles expression in English words . . . The native words I have chosen seem to me to have in them much of the striking quality of Australian primevalism." (For this detailed information about the first use of "Jindyworobak," I am indebted to John Tregenza, *Australian Little Magazines 1923-1954* (Adelaide: Libraries Board of South Australia, 1964.)

65. John Douglas Pringle, *Australian Accent* (London, 1958), p. 143. Pringle is citing poet-critic-biographer Frederick T. Macartney *(Australian Literary Studies, Sydney, 1957)*, who was among the first lecturers on Australian literature. (A good discussion of the Penguins is in Max Harris, "Conflicts in Australian Intellectual Life 1940-1964," *Literary Australia* (Melbourne, 1966), pp. 16-33. Mr. Harris, poet and a perceptive critic, was an editor of the *Angry Penguins* magazine, and a leader in the movement.

66. From "Batrachic Ode," one of sixteen poems included in a special Ern Malley issue of the *Angry Penguins* magazine (Autumn, 1944). The poems were concocted by poets James McAuley and Harold Stewart by "opening books at random, choosing a word or phrase haphazardly . . . misquoting," and the like. Why? The poets had regarded The Penguins as an Australian example of the modern movement in America and England which seemed to "render its devotees insensible of absurdity and incapable of ordinary discrimination." (The Ern Malley poems and a comment about the episode has been published as *Ern Malley's Poems,* with an introduction by Max Harris [Melbourne, 1961].)

67. Kenneth Slessor, "Australian Literature," *Southerly,* 1 (1945), pp. 34-35.

68. Max Harris, "Conflicts in Australian Intellectual Life 1940-1964" (see note 65), p. 23.

69. Kenneth Slessor, "Writing Poetry: The Why and the How," *Southerly,* 3 (1948), p. 169.

70. Evan Jones, "Australian Poetry Since 1920," *The Literature of Australia* (Ringwood, Victoria, Australia, 1964), pp. 125-26. Jones is citing Max Harris.

71. Kenneth Slessor, "Modern English Poetry," mimeographed manuscript of the minutes of a meeting in Sydney of the Australian English Association on September 17, 1931, which incorporates a paper read to the group by Mr. Slessor. (The paper, though entitled "Modern English Poetry," is introduced in the minutes as: "An interesting paper on 'Experiments in Modern English Poetry' was read . . ."). Footnote reference is to the third paragraph. One copy

of the manuscript is in the possession of Walter Stone of Cremorne, New South Wales, Australia, and another in the possession of the author. A printed version of Mr. Slessor's paper ("Modern English Poetry," Australian-English Association, Sydney: Offprint 9, October, 1931) is on file at the Mitchell Library in Sydney. Also, see note at end of bibliography.

72. His poems are published in the United States by Viking, New York.

73. This is from a line in A. D. Hope's "Australia" in which the poet, after being critical of his country ("A Nation of trees, drab green and desolate grey . . . the last of lands, the emptiest,") still turns "gladly home" to the possibilities and potentials of Australia.

74. A. D. Hope, *Australian Literature 1950-1962* (Melbourne: Melbourne University Press, 1963), p. 1. This is a 21-page pamphlet.

75. Judith Wright, "Inheritance and Discovery in Australian Poetry," *Literary Australia* (Melbourne, 1966), p. 7.

76. *Ibid.*, p. 8.

77. Quoted from the mimeographed copy of the AEA minutes in which is incorporated Slessor's address on "Modern English Poetry."

Chapter Two

1. Cited as part of a full page of testimonials included in the second issue of *Vision* (August, 1923). Jack Lindsay, Slessor's co-editor, in his autobiography, *The Roaring Twenties*, also recalls the success of the first issues of *Vision* (pp. 83-93). So does Jack's younger brother, Phil, in his autobiography, *I'd Live the Same Life Over* (London, 1941). Phil remembers, p. 107: "Nobody was more astounded than we by its instantaneous success. The first number was exhausted before it had finished printing; and we felt that literature had finally run up its Jolly Rogers in Australia, defying the puritanical Press."

2. Edited by Jack Lindsay and Kenneth Slessor; Sydney: The Vision Press.

3. London: Fanfrolico Press. Fanfrolico started in Sydney by bibliophile Jack Kirtley, with the assistance of Jack and Philip Lindsay and Slessor. Handprinting on handmade paper, Fanfrolico first published, in a limited edition illustrated with original wood engravings by Norman Lindsay, two volumes of poetry: Jack Lindsay's *Fauns and Ladies* and Ken Slessor's *Thief of the Moon*. When Jack Lindsay left for London in 1926, so did Kirtley and Fanfrolico, and from there Fanfrolico published Slessor's *Earth-Visitors*.

4. Jack Lindsay, *The Roaring Twenties*, p. 96. Jack Lindsay, in a letter to the author (undated and mailed in June, 1968 from Essex,

England), feels that "[Slessor] owed his drive to the *Vision* dynamics. (His verse before that was excellent, but rather static) . . . Right from the start, of course, he had a fine sense of diction, and his own view of things. What *Vision* did, I feel, was to *release* him."

5. *Vision*, II, August, 1923. See note 1.

6. Jack Lindsay, "Australian Poetry and Nationalism," *Vision*, I (May, 1923), p. 35.

7. *Ibid.*, p. 34.

8. *Ibid.*, p. 34.

9. Norman Lindsay's "proclamation of artistic consciousness." This is Slessor's phrase, used in his homage to Lindsay in *Southerly*, 1, 1959. *Creative Effort* was published in Sydney, 1920.

10. Jack Lindsay, *The Roaring Twenties*, p. 56. Slessor married in 1922, when he was twenty-one. It was a meaningful marriage, lasting until Noela's death in 1945, and it was "To Noela" that the poet dedicated his major volume, *One Hundred Poems* in 1944. He was to publish only three short poems after her death, changing the dedication in his final volume *Poems* (1957), to his second wife, Pauline, and to his son, Paul, born of this marriage. This second marriage was dissolved in 1961.

11. Kenneth Slessor, interview with John Thompson, p. 191.

12. See Chapter 1, note 71.

13. Kenneth Slessor, in copy under "The Norman Lindsay Number," *Southerly*, 1, 1959, frontispiece. Slessor opens his own article, "Australian Poetry and Norman Lindsay," p. 10, with: "It would be almost impossible, I think, to give any accurate idea of the course of poetry in Australia without saying something about [Norman Lindsay]."

14. Reprinted in *Southerly*, 1, 1959, as "Australian Poetry and Norman Lindsay," p. 10.

15. *Ibid.*, pp. 12-13.

16. *Ibid.*, p. 12.

17. *Ibid.*, p. 12.

18. *Ibid.*, p. 12.

19. Chris Wallace-Crabbe, "Kenneth Slessor and the Powers of Language," *The Literature of Australia*, ed. Geoffrey Dutton (Ringwood, Victoria, Australia, 1964), p. 342.

20. *Vision*, a literary quarterly, ran only to four issues: May, 1923; August, 1923; November, 1923; and February, 1924. In the February issue, there was an announcement of "The New Vision, Double the Size and Half the Price, Out in March, 1924 and Every 6 Weeks." But the success of the first issues which had prompted the announcement did not extend to the "New Vision"; in fact, the "New Vision" never appeared. Insufficient capital and insufficient men to produce

quality work on so large a scale in so short a time killed the "New Vision" as well as the old one. Yet Frank Johnson, the business head and printer of the Lindsay-Slessor-Johnson trio responsible for *Vision*, rallied to produce the *Vision* anthology, *Poetry in Australia* (Sydney, 1923).

21. R. G. Howarth, "Sound in Slessor's Poetry," *Southerly*, 4 (1955), p. 189.

22. Kenneth Slessor, letter to author, June 3, 1968. The full quote: "I have always been more concerned with aural effect rather than the 'pictorial sense,' and since this was a fundamental technical effort it did not come as a development." (The author had inquired whether the maturing poet had become "increasingly concerned with the music of the poem as well as its pictorial sense.")

23. Howarth, p. 189.

24. This is Slessor's expression in the interview with John Thompson (see note 11), *Southerly*, 3 (1966), p. 192. After acknowledging Tennyson as his master, he says: "I can't think of any masterpiece of music in words since Christopher Marlowe to compare with Tennyson's 'Tithonus.'"

25. From "Taoist," p. 6 of *Poems;* "plump cherubim" from "Rubens' Innocents," p. 7; strange riders "in dark furs," from "Earth-Visitors," p. 1. *Poems* is the definitive volume, incorporating all of Slessor's separate collections, including *Earth-Visitors*.

26. From "Marco-Polo," p. 8.

27. From "Winter Dawn," p. 14.

28. From "Adventure Bay," p. 30.

29. From "Heine in Paris," p. 11.

30. Lecture, 1954, was first published in *Southerly*, 2, 1955, and reprinted for special "Norman Lindsay Number," celebrating Lindsay's eightieth birthday. Reference is to this special issue: Kenneth Slessor, "Australian Poetry and Norman Lindsay," *Southerly*, 1 (1959), p. 13. Slessor, incidentally was editor of *Southerly* at this time, his editorship covering the years from 1956 to 1961.

31. Jack Lindsay, *Life Rarely Tells* (London, 1958), pp. 174-75.

32. Reprinted in *Earth-Visitors* as all ten *Vision* poems. "The Man of Sentiment" appeared in two issues: Part One in the first issue, May; Part Two in the second issue, August.

33. Jack Lindsay, *Life Rarely Tells,* Chapter 22, "Springwood," beginning on page 174, offers, in part, a vivid portrait of Norman Lindsay.

34. In an introduction to Norman's volume of *Pen Drawings*, 1931, his brother, Lionel, wrote: "Norman Lindsay believes in life—*la sacre vie*. Incessantly he has chanted his credo with his pen, that wonderful pen which seems to think on paper." Slessor quoted this with approval

in his article on Lindsay in *Southerly*, 1, 1959. The Lindsays, incidentally, are one of Australia's most famous artistic families.

35. *Poems*, the definitive collection, is a reprinting of *One Hundred Poems* with three short poems, "Polarities," "An Inscription for Dog River," and "Beach Burial" added. (See Chronology, 1957.)

36. *The Roaring Twenties*, p. 84.

37. *Ibid.*, p. 84.

38. *Ibid.*, p. 55.

39. *Southerly*, 3 (1966), pp. 194-95.

40. *A History of Australian Literature* (Sydney, 1961), p. 857.

41. *The Roaring Twenties*, p. 55.

42. Appearance in *Vision:* I, May, 1923 ("Thief of the Moon," "Rubens' Innocents," "January 18, 1922," and "The Man of Sentiment," Part One); II, August, 1923 ("New Magic," "Thieves' Kitchen," and "The Man of Sentiment," Part Two); III, November, 1923 ("Adventure Bay," "The Mask," "Good-night!"); and IV, February, 1924 ("The Embarkation for Cythera").

43. Sydney, 1923, ed. Jack Lindsay and Kenneth Slessor. Of the *Vision* poems, Slessor left out only "January 18, 1922" and "New Magic." To the *Vision* poems he added "A Surrender," "Mangroves," "Incongruity," "Pan at Lane Cove," "Nuremberg," and "The Ghost," all of which, except "Incongruity," he was to hold for his definitive collection, *Poems*.

44. "Incongruity" appears in *Poetry in Australia*, p. 56, and is included in *Earth-Visitors*, p. 25, but is excluded from *Poems*.

45. In *One Hundred Poems* (Sydney, 1944), in which Slessor brings together poems from the *Earth-Visitors* collection, as well as the two subsequent ones, *Cuckooz Contrey* and *Five Bells*, the poet says *OHP* "is divided into three chronological stages," and he assigns the *Earth-Visitors* poems to the years of 1919-1926.

46. Several had been published previously in *Thief of the Moon* (Sydney, 1924). This was "privately" printed and limited in edition to one hundred signed copies. Quoting from a note in the 51-page volume: "This is . . . issued to subscribers from the Hand-press of J. T. Kirtley. Set in type and printed on handmade paper at 28 Burton Street, Kirribilli Sydney."

47. Max Harris, p. 11. (See Chapter 1, note 12.)

48. *Ibid*, p. 11.

49. Judith Wright, "Kenneth Slessor—Romantic and Modern," *Preoccupations in Australian Poetry* (Melbourne: Oxford University Press, 1965), p. 141.

50. *Ibid.*, p. 145.

51. In *Earth-Visitors*, Rapptown was Bargo. Slessor changed it "to avoid identification with the near-Sydney town of Bargo, once a

small country district, now almost a metropolitan suburb. 'Rapptown' is an invented general name, is in the spirit of small Australian (and American) town-names and cannot be identified with any specific place." (Letter to author, June 3, 1968.)

52. Chris Wallace-Crabbe, "Kenneth Slessor and the Powers of Language," pp. 345-46. (See note 19.)

53. Kenneth Slessor, "Writing Poetry: The Why and the How," p. 169.

54. *Ibid.*, p. 167.

55. *Ibid.*, p. 168.

56. *Ibid.*, p. 169.

57. The poem on page 36 of *Poems* has "Girls with *apple-eyes* are flying," and there is no separation between the lines "Riding on a tide of country faces" and "Up and down the smoke and crying." Here the poem has been quoted precisely as Slessor quoted it in his "Writing Poetry: The Why and the How."

Slessor made similar changes in other poems from the *Earth-Visitors* collection. Originally, for example, the fourth line in the title poem was "Princes gone wenching, barons with sable masks." This became in *One Hundred Poems* and *Poems:* "Princes gone feasting, barons with gipsy eyes." Similarly, in line 32, "To clash the wench's mind . . ." became "To vex a farm girl. . . ." A few other such changes include "wenches" to "dancers" in line 27 of "Realities," "In phosphor-green and gules and flame" to "Scaly with poison, bright with flame" in the first line of "Pan at Lane Cove," and "presst" to "pressed" in line 24 of "The Ghost" and line 10 of "Undine," and "magik" to the less exotic "magic" in line 2 of "Undine." The reason for the changes? Slessor, in a letter to the author, June 3, 1968, says: "changes in the text of poems in later editions were caused by a desire to eliminate youthful affectations and mock Elizabethan archaisms (e.g., "wenches" and "wenching," "magick" and "fantastick"), precious decoration ("sable masks" and "gules") and special "poetic" language (e.g. "fruitage"). [Slessor had first used "fruitage," not "harvest," in the second line of "Stars."] I also tried to avoid the "poetic" spellings imitated from Jack Lindsay in *Vision* (e.g., "presst" for "pressed") though I suspect there is perhaps a slight case to be argued for the staccato whip of the "t" ending in past participles where there is a sound effect that differs (to my ear at least) from the less decisive "ed" ending.

58. "Writing Poetry: The Why and the How," p. 169.

59. *Ibid.*, p. 169.

60. *Ibid.*, p. 170.

61. *Ibid.*, p. 170.

62. T. Inglis Moore, "Kenneth Slessor," *Southerly*, 4 (1947), p. 199.

63. "Music," VIII: p. 30; "Clocks" is not included in *Poems*; Nuremburg: p. 3.

64. Max Harris, *Kenneth Slessor*, pp. 18 and 6.

65. From "William Street" *(Five Bells)*, p. 99.

66. Interview with John Thompson, p. 195.

Chapter Three

1. H. M. Green, *Modern Australian Poetry* (Melbourne: Melbourne University Press, 1946), introductory to first edition, p. vii.

2. *Cuckooz Contrey* (Sydney: Frank Johnson, 1932), 76 pages.

3. Max Harris, *Kenneth Slessor*, p. 16.

4. Letter from Slessor to author, June 3, 1968.

5. *Ibid.*

6. Kenneth Slessor, "Modern English Poetry," manuscript, p. 5. Copy in possession of author and another in possession of Walter Stone of Cremorne, New South Wales. Printed version (Sydney: Australian-English Association, Offprint 9, October, 1931) is on file at the Mitchell Library in Sydney. (See note 71, Chapter 1.)

7. Joseph Wood Krutch, *The Modern Temper*, New York, Harcourt, Brace & World, Inc., 1956, p. 52.

8. Slessor to Jaffa, June 3, 1968.

9. Selden Rodman, *One Hundred Modern Poems* (New York, 1953), in introduction, under section "Revolution of the Word," p. xxi.

10. *Australian Encyclopedia* (Sydney, 1963), V, 332.

11. Kenneth Slessor, "Modern English Poetry," manuscript (see note 6), p. 1.

12. *Ibid.*, p. 1.

13. *Ibid.*, p. 1.

14. *Ibid.*, p. 1.

15. *Ibid.*, p. 2.

16. *Ibid.*, p. 2.

17. *Ibid.*, p. 3.

18. *Ibid.*, p. 3.

19. "Poetry in Australia—Kenneth Slessor," *Southerly*, 3 (1966), p. 192.

20. "Modern English Poetry," p. 5 (see note 6).

21. *Ibid.*, p. 6.

22. Slessor, "Writing Poetry: The Why and the How," p. 168; "Poetry in Australia—Kenneth Slessor," pp. 193-94.

23. "Modern English Poetry," p. 2.

24. "Poetry in Australia—Kenneth Slessor," p. 194.

25. *Southerly,* 3 (1948), p. 167.

26. "English Project 3," *Sydney Daily Telegraph,* Monday, July 24, 1967, p. 16, col. 2.

27. Slessor quoted in *Walkabout,* October 1, 1952, on "Our Authors' Page." *(Walkabout* is a *Life*-sized monthly published in Melbourne. The title "signifies a racial characteristic of the aborigine who is always on the move. The magazine takes readers on a walkabout through Australia and its territories"—quoted from magazine contents page.)

28. *Southerly,* 3 (1948), pp. 167 and 171.

29. Max Harris, *Kenneth Slessor,* p. 10.

30. Quoted by Richard Ellmann and Charles Feidelson, Jr., in *The Modern Tradition* (New York: Oxford University Press, 1965), p. vi.

31. *Ibid.,* p. vii.

32. Quoted by Cyril Connolly in *The Modern Movement* (New York: Atheneum, 1966), p. 3.

33. He was actually president of the club from 1956 to 1964. Max Harris, in *Kenneth Slessor* (see note 3), says, "The creation of a lush, affluent parochial home for newspapermen largely came about through Slessor's patriarchal interest and administrative pertinacity" (p. 1).

34. Jack Lindsay, *The Roaring Twenties,* p. 203 and chapters 5 and 8.

35. *Ibid.,* pp. 116-17.

36. George Blaikie, pp. 50-51.

37. A merchant with a full sense of life, whose *Memoirs* of the pleasures of India in the mid-eighteenth century, inspired Slessor.

38. Jack Lindsay, *The Roaring Twenties,* p. 196.

39. Camus says in L'Été: "In the midst of winter, I finally learned that there was in me an invincible summer." Also, Albert Maquet's critical biography (New York: George Braziller, 1958) is entitled *Albert Camus, The Invincible Summer.*

40. Rieux is Camus's narrator in *The Plague.*

41. H. M. Green, *A History of Australian Literature* (Sydney, 1961), II, p. 861.

42. Jack Lindsay, *The Roaring Twenties,* p. 55. Lindsay recalls meeting Slessor: "We talked in a flat he had on the North Shore, right over the harbour's waters. . . . The waters of the harbour briskly moving in regular scalloped lines like a child's painting of the sea—if the child were working with a brush dabbed in blue fire. Enclosing us with a busy tangle of lights." Poet Douglas Stewart, a friend, sees Slessor "as a poet at a tower window, sometimes staring down at the water and grinning wryly at his reflection, sometimes gazing out to

the blue horizon beyond the Heads and seeing the wraiths of the great voyagers." ("Harbour and Ocean," *The Flesh and the Spirit* [Sydney, 1948], p. 161.) References to windows, panes, and glass through which one peers are many in Slessor's poems. The poet, himself, in "Winter Dawn," "rub[s] on the smoking pane/A port to sea"; the ghost in "The Ghost" is "pressed to the dark pane"; the "shining Guest" (in "Music" XII) has "His face like a strange wafer pressed/Secret and starry, at thy pane," etc.

43. E.g., "Adventure Bay."

44. From "Five Bells" *(Five Bells)*, p. 103.

45. Judith Wright, *Preoccupations in Australian Poetry* (Melbourne: Oxford University Press, 1965), p. 144.

46. Chris Wallace-Crabbe, "Kenneth Slessor and the Powers of Language," p. 348.

47. Slessor says: "It is a fact that Cook was stabbed with an English knife that had been traded to the Hawaiian natives only a few days before. ("English Project 3," *Sydney Daily Telegraph*, Monday, July 24, 1967.)

48. Charles Higham, "The Poetry of Kenneth Slessor," *Quadrant* (December, 1959), p. 71.

49. Kenneth Slessor, "Modern English Poetry," manuscript. (See note 6.)

50. *Southerly*, 3 (1948), p. 167.

51. "Kenneth Slessor and the Powers of Language," p. 350.

52. Kenneth Slessor, "English Project 3," *Sydney Daily Telegraph*, Monday, July 24, 1967, p. 16.

53. *Ibid.*, p. 16.

54. *Ibid.*, p. 16.

55. *Ibid.*, p. 16. Sir Isaac Newton suggested a new way, by the comparison of two clocks, one marking Greenwich time and the other the local time by the sun at sea. The great problem was to construct a clock which would keep absolutely accurate time through the vast range of temperature and humidity of a sea voyage. Two famous English watchmakers supplied the chronometers for this historic experiment. One was made by John Arnold, the other by Larcum Kendal from a prototype invented by John Harrison.

Chapter Four

1. "English Project—No. 4," *Sydney Daily Telegraph*, Monday, July 31, 1967, p. 16.

2. *Ibid.*

3. *Ibid.*

4. *Ibid.*

5. *Ibid.*

6. Second line of poem, p. 103.

7. Slessor says "I have lived many lives. "—line 6 of the first verse. This is not rhetoric. As Max Harris indicates *(Kenneth Slessor,* p. 27), "His poetry is the reliving of many lives."

8. Sydney: Angus & Robertson, 1939.

9. *Poems,* of course, is Slessor's last book, but it is essentially *One Hundred Poems,* with thirty lines added. (Of course, though, some of these lines belong to the beautiful elegy "Beach Burial.")

10. From *Cuckooz Contrey:* page 68 in *Poems.*

11. Douglas Stewart, "Harbour and Ocean," *The Flesh and The Spirit* (Sydney, 1948), p. 157.

12. See p. 105; also note 52, Chapter 3.

13. "English Project—No. 4."

14. *Ibid.*

15. *Ibid.*

16. *Ibid.*

17. Reprinted in *Southerly,* 3 (1966), p. 196.

18. Philip Lindsay, *I'd Live the Same Life Over,* quoted by Jack Lindsay in *The Roaring Twenties,* p. 195.

19. T. Inglis Moore, "Kenneth Slessor," *Southerly,* 4 (1947), p. 201.

20. Hugh McCrae, *Story-Book Only* (Sydney: Angus and Robertson, 1948), p. 118.

21. Max Harris, *Kenneth Slessor,* p. 25.

22. *Sydney Daily Telegraph,* Monday, July 31, 1967, p. 16, col 7.

23. *Ibid.*

24. *Ibid.*

25. McCrae, p. 120.

26. In many ways, the spirit of affirmation and gaiety in McCrae's *Satyrs and Sunlight* (1910), filled the first page of *Vision* a decade later. Slessor was very fond and appreciative of McCrae (see Slessor's "Australian Poetry and Hugh McCrae," *Southerly,* 3, 1956).

27. "Shang Ya! I want to be your friend," cries the young man in "The Old Play" (from *Cuckooz Contrey,* p. 80 in *Poems),* Slessor's not particularly successful poem-series about the gods watching man perform his old play of life. Friendship is important, for time-life ultimately separates man. "The Old Play," apart from its being another expression of Slessor's sometimes seeing life as performance (e.g., "Theatre of Varieties" in "Next Turn," p. 29 in *Poems),* is interesting in its movement between stage and audience, between actors (man) and audience (gods). Yet, the poem seems somewhat contrived, and though composed during Slessor's middle period, recalls some of the artificiality of the earliest one.

28. A. D. Hope (1907-   ) has written of "The Wandering Islands"

and Christopher Brennan (1870-1932) of "The Wanderer." The sense of moving through life, alone and apart, unable to make contact, is often expressed in Australian poetry.

29. Reprinted in *Southerly*, 3 (1966), p. 196.

30. Jack Lindsay, *The Roaring Twenties*, p. 196.

31. For clarification at this point: numbers in parentheses refer to pages in *Poems* (see beginning of "Notes and References"). *Poems*, Slessor's last volume, is essentially a reprint of *One Hundred Poems* with three poems added. There is some slight but not significant shifting of poems from *OHP* to *P*, e.g., "A Surrender" is placed after "Winter Dawn," becoming the twelfth poem in the volume, where previously it had been the fifteenth, after "Thieves Kitchen"; "Metempsychosis" and "Mephistopheles Perverted" are moved up one position, and so on.

32. T. Inglis Moore, *Southerly*, 4 (1947), p. 201.

33. "English Project—No. 4."

34. "Writing Poetry: The Why and the How," *Southerly*, 3 (1948), p. 171.

35. "English Project—No. 4."

36. Quoted in R. M. Crawford, *An Australian Perspective* (Madison: The University of Wisconsin Press, 1960), p. 40.

37. From "Talbingo" in *Cuckooz Contrey*, p. 70 in *Poems*.

38. From "Winter Dawn" in *Earth-Visitors*, p. 14 in *Poems*.

39. From "Music," sequence IV, in *Earth-Visitors*, p. 35 in *Poems*.

40. From "Crow Country," in *Cuckooz Contrey*, p. 69 in *Poems*.

41. From "Country Towns" in *Cuckooz Contrey*, p. 71 in *Poems*.

42. "English Project—No. 4."

43. R. G. Howarth, "Sound in Slessor's Poetry," *Southerly*, 4 (1955), p. 190. Reprinted from a Commonwealth Literary Fund Lecture at the University of Western Australia in 1952.

44. *Ibid.*, p. 190.

45. *A Short History of Australia* (New York: New American Library, 1963), p. 33.

46. "English Project—No. 4."

47. *Ibid.*

Selected Bibliography

PRIMARY SOURCES

Slessor's Poems
(in chronological order)

Vision: A Literary Quarterly. Sydney: The Vision Press, I, May, 1923; II, August, 1923; III, November, 1923; IV, February, 1924. Edited by Jack Lindsay and Kenneth Slessor.

Poetry in Australia 1923. Sydney: The Vision Press, 1923. Edited by Jack ˙Lindsay and Kenneth Slessor. Preface by Norman Lindsay.

Thief of the Moon. Sydney: Hand press of J. T. Kirtley, 1924. Woodcuts by Norman Lindsay. Edition limited to subscribers.

Earth-Visitors. London: Fanfrolico Press, 1926. Woodcuts and copperplate engravings by Norman Lindsay. Includes several poems from *Thief of the Moon.* Public but limited edition.

Cuckooz Contrey. Sydney: Frank Johnson, 1932. Etching by Norman Lindsay. Public but limited edition.

Five Bells. Sydney: Frank Johnson, 1939. Drawings by Norman Lindsay. Public but limited edition.

One Hundred Poems, 1919-1939. Sydney: Angus and Robertson, 1944. The collected work: twenty-five of the thirty-six poems in *Earth-Visitors* and the poems of *Cuckooz Contrey* and *Five Bells.*

Poems. Sydney: Angus and Robertson, 1957. (Sirius edition, 1964, used.) Essentially a reissue of *One Hundred Poems* with three short poems added.

Other

Trio (A Book of Poems). Sydney: The Sunnybrook Press, 1931. "Five Visions of Captain Cook" and poems by Harley Matthews and Colin Simpson. Drawings and designs by Raymond Lindsay (Jack's brother), William E. Pidgeon, James E. Flett, and George Finey. A map by James Emery.

Slessor's Papers, Lectures, Articles, Interviews
(in chronological order)

"Modern English Poetry." Paper presented to the Australian-English Association, Sydney, September 17, 1931. Mimeographed manuscript held by author and Walter Stone of Cremorne, New South Wales. Modified version reproduced as Offprint 9, October, 1931, of the Australian-English Association.

"Australian Literature," *Southerly,* 1 (1945), pp. 31-36. Text of an address given at the Twenty-first Anniversary Dinner of the Australian English Association on November 23, 1944.

"Writing Poetry: The Why and the How," *Southerly* 3 (1948), pp. 161-71. Text of one of a series of broadcasts conducted by the Australian Broadcasting Commission and arranged by John Thompson of ABC, himself a poet.

"Australian Poetry and Hugh McCrae," *Southerly,* 3 (1956), pp. 128-37. Text from a Commonwealth Literary Fund Lecture delivered at the University of Sydney in September, 1954.

"Australian Authors Reply to Their English Critics: A Controversy," *Australian Letters,* I, 1 (June, 1957), p. 18.

"Australian Poetry and Norman Lindsay," *Southerly,* 1 (1959), pp. 10-16. Text is revised and condensed from a Commonwealth Literary Fund Lecture, 1954, which was first published in *Southerly,* 2 (1955).

"Poetry in Australia—Kenneth Slessor," *Southerly,* 3 (1966), pp. 190-98. Text of television interview conducted by John Thompson and the Australian Broadcasting Commission, November 7, 1962.

"English Project," *Sydney Daily Telegraph,* Monday, July 10, 1967-Monday, August 21, 1967, a five-part series written by Slessor discussing Australian poetry being studied in the secondary schools of New South Wales. In "English Project 3," Monday, July 24, and "English Project—No. 4," Monday, July 31, Slessor discussed his own work. In the first he devoted the entire article to "Five Visions of Captain Cook," and in the second he divided it among "Five Bells," "Country Towns," "North Country," "South Country," "William Street," "Sleep," and "Beach Burial."

Letter to Author (Slessor to Jaffa), dated June 3, 1968, dealing with reasons for changes in later editions of poems, relationship to Eliot's verse, technical purposes, and so on.

SECONDARY SOURCES

Australian Encyclopedia, V. Sydney: The Grolier Society, 1965.
Unsigned. "Australian Official War Correspondent Mr. Kenneth

Slessor Has Lodged Resignation with War Cabinet," (Headline developed from lead sentence.) *Melbourne Herald,* February 24, 1944.

BLAIKIE, GEORGE. *Remember Smith's Weekly.* Adelaide: Rigby, 1966.

BUCKLEY, VINCENT. "Kenneth Slessor: Realist or Romantic?," *Essays in Poetry, Mainly Australian.* Melbourne: Melbourne University Press, 1957, pp. 111-21.

CAMUS, ALBERT. *The Plague.* New York: Alfred A. Knopf, 1958.

_____. "L'Eté" (Return to Tipasa), *Lyrical and Critical Essays,* tr. Ellen Conroy Kennedy; ed., Philip Thody. New York: Alfred A. Knopf, 1968.

CONNOLLY, CYRIL, *The Modern Movement.* New York: Atheneum, 1966.

CRAWFORD, R. M. *An Australian Perspective.* Madison: The University of Wisconsin Press, 1960.

ELLMAN, RICHARD and CHARLES FEIDELSON, JR. *The Modern Tradition.* New York: Oxford University Press, 1965.

GREEN, H. M. *Modern Australian Poetry.* Melbourne: Melbourne University Press, 1946, introductory to first edition, specifically p. vii.

_____. *Australian Literature 1900-1950.* Melbourne: Melbourne University Press, 1951. A 64-page pamphlet "published for the Trustees of The Public Library of Victoria." Not to be confused with the major work, *A History of Australian Literature.*

_____. *A History of Australian Literature* (2 vols.). Sydney: Angus and Robertson, 1961, particularly vol. II, pp. 845-54; 855-68.

HARRIS, MAX. *Kenneth Slessor.* Melbourne: Lansdowne Press, 1963. A pamphlet (48 pages) in the *Australian Writers and Their Work* series, under the general editorship of Geoffrey Dutton.

_____. "Conflicts in Australian Intellectual Life 1940-1964," *Literary Australia.* Melbourne: F. W. Cheshire, 1966, pp. 16-33.

HIGHAM, CHARLES. "The Poetry of Kenneth Slessor," *Quadrant* (December, 1959), pp. 65-73.

HOPE, A. D. *Australian Literature 1950-1962.* Melbourne: Melbourne University Press, 1963. A 21-page pamphlet.

_____. *Collected Poems 1930-1965.* New York: The Viking Press, 1966.

HOWARTH, R. G. "Sound in Slessor's Poetry," *Southerly,* 4 (1955), pp. 189-96. (Reprinted from a Commonwealth Literary Fund Lecture at the University of Western Australia in 1952.)

INGAMELLS, REX, ed. *Jindyworobak Anthology, 1947.* Melbourne: Jindyworobak Publications, 1947.

JONES, EVAN. "Australian Poetry Since 1920," *The Literature of Australia,* ed. Geoffrey Dutton. Ringwood, Victoria, Australia: Penguin Books 1964, pp. 100-133.

KEESING, NANCY and DOUGLAS STEWART, ed. *Old Bush Songs and Australian Bush Ballads.* Sydney: Angus and Robertson, 1955.

LINDSAY, JACK. "Australian Poetry and Nationalism," *Vision: A Literary Quarterly,* I (May, 1923), pp. 30-35. (Co-editor with Slessor of the four issues.)

————. *Poetry in Australia 1923.* Sydney: The Vision Press, December, 1923. Co-editor with Slessor.

————. *Life Rarely Tells.* London: The Bodley Head, 1958.

————. *The Roaring Twenties.* London: The Bodley Head, 1960.

LINDSAY, PHILIP. *I'd Live the Same Life Over.* London: Hutchinson & Co., 1941.

MAQUET, ALBERT. *Albert Camus: The Invincible Summer.* New York: George Braziller, 1958.

MATTHEWS, JOHN PENGWERNE. *Tradition in Exile.* Melbourne: F. W. Cheshire (in association with University of Toronto Press), 1962.

McCRAE, HUGH. *Story-Book Only.* Angus and Robertson: Sydney, 1948.

MOORE, T. INGLIS. "Kenneth Slessor," *Southerly,* 4 (1947), pp. 194-205.

————, ed. *Poetry in Australia,* I, From the Ballads to Brennan. Berkeley and Los Angeles: University of California Press, 1964, introduction, particularly pp. xxi-xxxi. First published, Sydney: Angus and Robertson, 1964.

————, ed. *Henry Kendall (Australian Poets).* Sydney: Angus and Robertson, 1963.

MUDIE, IAN and COLIN THIELE, ed. *Australian Poets Speak.* Adelaide: Rigby, 1961.

PALMER, NETTIE. *Modern Australian Literature (1900-1923).* Melbourne and Sydney: Lothian Book Publishing Co., 1924.

PALMER, VANCE. *The Legend of the Nineties.* Melbourne: Melbourne University Press, 1954.

PHILLIPS, A. A., "The Cultural Cringe," *Meanjin,* IV (1950), p. 299.

————, ed. *Bernard O'Dowd (Australian Poets).* Sydney: Angus and Robertson, 1963.

PRINGLE, JOHN DOUGLAS. *Australian Accent.* London: Chatto and Windus, 1958.

RODMAN, SELDEN. *One Hundred Modern Poems.* New York: New American Library, 1953. The introduction (pp. vii-xxx, particularly the section, "Revolution of the word") is relevant, as is

Part II of the anthology, "Forerunners" where Slessor's "Five Bells" appears on page 91.

SEMMLER, CLEMENT. *Kenneth Slessor.* London: Longmans, Green & Co., 1966. A pamphlet (44 pages) in the *Writers and Their Work* series of the British Council and National Book League, under the general editorship of Geoffrey Bullough.

SHAPCOTT, THOMAS. "Slessor's Poetry," *The Bulletin* (January 28, 1957), p. 17.

SLESSOR, KENNETH. "Our Authors Page" (by Rex Ingamells), *Walkabout* (October 1, 1952), unnumbered page.

STEWART, DOUGLAS. "Harbour and Ocean," *The Flesh and the Spirit.* Sydney: Angus and Robertson, 1948, pp. 157-63.

————, ed. *Poetry in Australia*, II. Modern Australian Verse, Berkeley and Los Angeles: University of California Press, 1964, particularly p. xxx. First published, Sydney: Angus and Robertson, 1964.

THOMPSON, JOHN. "Poetry in Australia—Kenneth Slessor," text of television interview over Australian Broadcasting Commission, *Southerly*, 3 (1966), pp. 190-98.

TREGENZA, JOHN. *Australian Little Magazines 1923-1954.* Adelaide: Libraries Board of South Australia, 1964.

WALLACE-CRABBE, CHRIS. "Kenneth Slessor and the Powers of Language," *The Literature of Australia*, ed. Geoffrey Dutton. Ringwood, Victoria, Australia: Penguin Books, 1964, pp. 342-52.

WARD, RUSSEL. *Australia.* Englewood Cliffs, New Jersey: Prentice-Hall 1965, pp. 1-37 and 77-100 in particular.

————, ed. *The Penguin Book of Australian Ballads.* Ringwood, Victoria, Australia: Penguin Books, 1964.

WRIGHT, JUDITH. "Kenneth Slessor-Romantic and Modern," *Preoccupations in Australian Poetry.* Melbourne: Oxford University Press, 1965, pp. 140-50.

————. "Inheritance and Discovery in Australian Poetry," *Literary Australia.* Melbourne: F. W. Cheshire, 1966, pp. 1-15.

OTHER SOURCES

For General Reference and Background

AUCHTERLONIE, DOROTHY. *Australian Poetry 1968.* Sydney: Angus and Robertson, 1968.

BROWN, CYRIL. *Writings for Australia.* Melbourne: Hawthorn, 1956.

BUCKLEY, VINCENT. "Utopianism and Vitalism in Australian Literature," *Quadrant* (March, 1959), pp. 39-51.

CHRISTESEN, C. B. *On Native Grounds* (Australian Writing from *Meanjin Quarterly.* Sydney: Angus and Robertson, 1968.

DUTTON, GEOFFREY. "Australian Poetic Diction," *Australian Letters,* I, 1 (June, 1957), pp. 12-16.

————, ed. *The Literature of Australia.* Ringwood, Victoria: Penguin Books, 1964.

EWERS, J. K. *Creative Writing in Australia.* Melbourne: Georgian House, 1945.

FITZGERALD, ROBERT D. *Forty Years' Poems.* Sydney: Angus and Robertson, 1965.

GREEN, H. M. *Fourteen Minutes.* Sydney: Angus and Robertson, 1944. Based on radio talks for the Australian Broadcasting Commission in 1942.

HORNE, DONALD. *The Lucky Country (Australia Today).* Baltimore, Maryland: Penguin Books, 1965.

HOWARTH, R. G., KENNETH SLESSOR, and JOHN THOMPSON. *The Penguin Book of Modern Australian Verse.* Hammondsworth, Middlesex, England: Penguin Books, 1961.

JOHNSTON, GRAHAME. "The Language of Australian Literature," *Australian Literary Studies,* III, 1 (June, 1967), pp. 18-27. (*ALS* is edited by Dr. L. T. Hergenhan and published by the University of Tasmania.)

LINDSAY, NORMAN. *Bohemians of the Bulletin.* Sydney: Angus and Robertson, 1965.

MACKANESS, GEORGE. *Bibliomania (An Australian Book Collector's Essays).* Sydney: Angus and Robertson, 1965.

MACARTNEY, F. T. "The Poetry of Kenneth Slessor," *Meanjin* 3 (1957), pp. 265-72.

McAULEY, JAMES. *Captain Quiros.* Sydney: Angus and Robertson, 1964.

McCUAIG, RONALD. "Contemporary Australian Literature," *The Literary Review* (Australian Number), Winter, 1963-1964. *Review* is published quarterly by Fairleigh Dickinson University, New Jersey.

MILLER, E. MORRIS. *Australian Literature,* 2 vols. Melbourne: Melbourne University Press, 1940.

MITCHELL, A. C. W. "Kenneth Slessor and the Grotesque," *Australian Literary Studies,* I, 4 (December, 1964), pp. 242-50.

SLESSOR, KENNETH, ed. *Australian Poetry 1945.* Sydney: Angus and Robertson, 1945.

————. "The Anatomy of Anecdote," *The Etruscan,* XIII, 2 (June, 1964), pp. 16-18. (*The Etruscan* is a magazine of the Bank of New South Wales.)

SLESSOR, KENNETH and ROBERT WALKER. *Life at the Cross.* Adelaide: Rigby, 1965. (Slessor is responsible for the text, and Walker for the photographs in this picture book about King's Cross, Sydney's "Greenwich Village" area.)

STEPHENSEN, P. R. *Kookaburras and Satyrs*. (Some recollections of the Fanfrolico Press.) Cremorne, New South Wales, Australia: Talkarra Press (Handprinted by Walter W. Stone), 1954. Limited edition.

STEWART, DOUGLAS. *Collected Poems 1936-1967*. Sydney: Angus and Robertson, 1967.

WALLACE-CRABBE, CHRIS. *Six Voices (Contemporary Australian Poets)*. Sydney: Angus and Robertson, 1963.

WILLIS, DAVID K. "The New Australians: Migrants Bring Skills to Australia," *The Christian Science Monitor*, Friday, May 31, 1968, p. 2, cols. 1-3.

WRIGHT, JUDITH, ed. *New Land New Language*. Melbourne: Oxford University Press, 1957.

NOTE: Some essays on Slessor, not too accessible to the average reader, have been brought together in a single volume, *Critical Essays on Kenneth Slessor,* selected and with an introductory essay by A. K. Thomson, and recently published in Brisbane by The Jacaranda Press. Mr. Thomson also includes Slessor's paper, "Modern English Poetry," presented to the Australian English Association in 1931 and referred to in our study, and thus makes generally available an important document in the development of modern Australian poetry.

Index